BE THE FLAME NOT THE MOTH

Be The Flame
Not The Moth

An Anthology of Poems (and some prose) by

Alice Kelly Purnell

Be the Flame Not the Moth

An Anthology of Poems (and some prose) by

Alice Kelly Purnell

Hove Sussex. England September 2010

Published by the Golden Flower Press,
Belper, Derby, England

ISBN 978 09527988 1 1

DEDICATION

This book is dedicated to my wonderful friends and to my dear daughters Sara and Rebecca and to my grandchildren Tom, Joe, Eliza and Jake.

PREFACE

This is an anthology of poems written between 1982 and 2010 by Alice Kelly Purnell. Many are new and she has published some before in her three earlier publications:

"Bad Timing" 1989
"Sex & Chocolate" 1991
"I Wet Myself" 1993

ACKNOWLEDGEMENTS

She has retained some of the illustrations she used in these works by herself, and by Ben and Sara Purnell (now Candler), Ruth Jenkins & Judy Krolick, and again she thanks them. She also thanks her good friends Keith Rossetti and Jed Bland for computer & layout help, Thanks also to fellow poets Judy Krolick and Jill Longmate for proofing and suggestions.

Alice has found that writing brought laughter and could help work through many of the awful things of life, such as the mental illness and death of Ben (6/9/71 – 26/4/97,) for whom she wrote her Poems "For a Dead Son", which she places here chronologically, through his illness to the end. Writing poems helps deal with some very deep emotions: grief, loss, love or joy. It can be therapeutic; it can be great fun too!

Alice coped with divorce, but later the joy of some beautiful times of love. A joy that was followed after a few years by each lover eventually leaving her. Rejection really is tough, don't you know it? She cannot blame them. She says she is a deeply melancholic optimist, a quite hopeless combination. But her lasting joy has always been family, friends, Nature and learning -that never stops.

She was a founder of the Hove Women Writers Group, and remembers with a smile the many Port & Poetry evenings we organised. She also thanks the Brighton & Sussex Folk People, the musicians, singers and poets with whom she performed in local pubs and clubs, particularly Tim Kent and Sandra Goddard.

Alice is a retired registered nurse, particularly concerned with the care of the elderly. She works as a qualified psychologist counsellor. In her later years she fights the "delights" of acute osteoarthritis. Music and Palaeontology (she really likes ammonites) are her passions. She used to sing with Brighton Consort and the Brighton Festival Chorus, but as well as Early & Choral music, loves Jazz and Folk music. Music and poetry both can lift the heart.

We know that Laughter and tears are old companions. We need both sometimes.

In Eridoo Sumeria a message in cuneiform script, is written an inscription over five thousand years old.

It writes "To a Far off Place in a far off time … It is written still".

POEM THEME INDEX

CONCERNS

POEMS FOR A DEAD SON

Arranged chronologically
Ben 6/9/71 – 26/4/97

LOVE LOST & FOUND

LOVE FOUND

ALPHABETIC INDEX & PAGE

A CIRCLE DANCE

Bare legs, feet fly and touch the ground,
The woman - a girl in a flowing skirt.
She led. I held her left hand
And followed her lead;
No stranger to this dance.
The music played, the candle burnt.
A wondrous female energy this:
A circle made in eternity.

Bare legs, bare feet, toes touch toes,
The woman - a girl in my gentle arms.
I led; she held both my hands
And followed my lead;
A stranger to this dance.
The music played, the candle burnt.
A timeless and female lovemaking this:
A circle made for eternity.

Bare legs, bare breasts, skin touching.
I am a woman in her strong arms.
She led; I held both her breasts
And followed her lead;
Not strangers to this dance.
The music played, the candle burnt.
A too brief, but wonderful equality this,
A circle made by eternity.

Bare legs, bare souls, mind touches mind.
We are women in each other's arms.
No leader, each holds the other's body
Close and follows love's lead.
The music played, the candle burnt.
So natural is this dance
Exquisite excitement in this mutuality;
The circles of our nipples and lips.

A GRAVE MATTER

A grave matter
Is the graveyard.

Its gravity draws
Me to the ground;

A graven image
Of what is to be.

Gravel under my feet
Grinds me back to now,

Away from these
Stones.

Far from these
Bones.

Off I walk, wiser at
The deaths of these,

None known to me,
Who also stared in

Curiosity at stones,
And what was to be.

But
        Not
                Yet.

A POESY

On the Downs were cornflowers, cowslips,
Varied grasses, broom and thistle.

I picked a bunch to give to her. These
Wild flowers remind me of her laugh.

I took them to her, so natural were they.
The day was hot, and the flowers wilted.

I put damp grass round them, carried with
Care on my walk home to give to my love.

At her door, they were a sorry sight.
She took them none the less, and found a

Vase, arranged those dead flowers, weeds,
With the same love as I picked them.

A WOMAN'S TIME

Belly swollen still; blood on my legs,
My body, my heart rent, part of me gone.

Free now, but so weak, knees trembling,
Dizzy deep burning pain. The child is lost,

The woman, grown through this pain.
A life demands a death.

Pale slender fingers tremble as I move
My hands over my body, familiar and strange,

This thing nature had done to my body.
Against nature to lose, but freeing my nature

To be myself: so very alone now,
In this woman's time.

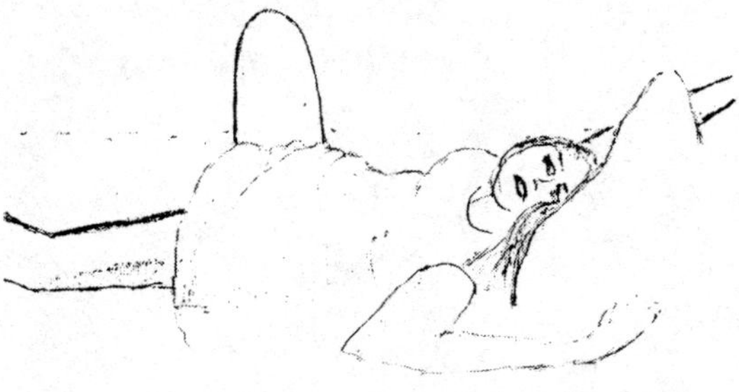

ACCESS DAY

They carry no cards, the Access Day People,
Divorced from their partner and family life.
Caught in a Court Order, snatching at love,
With their children who can't understand –
Doing Time as a "family" to serve the Court.
Official Mediation is a joke.

Resentment at talking to one, once loved.
Time Out with children, parenting is timed.
It's unreasonably short and unnaturally long:
Done to a Timetable, moments as "family"
Time to catch up on the time we have lost.
Just what is reasonable access?

Questions sought from the mouths of the children
A quest for the truth, it's done from a distance.
They don't know the answers, but feel the strain.
"How's your father," could be the question, or
"How is your mother?" he casually asks later on.
"The Ex" becomes the opposition.

"Are THEY quite happy? Somehow hoping for "No"
"What have you been doing" and "Been anywhere nice?"
"Tell me about you", "Are you OK? "School alright?"
"Know that I will always love you" my daughter or son.
"Know that I miss you", "Though you have gone away
"Know I am always here for you."

The family split-up is the hardest to bear for the one
Left alone, it is like a punishment for being cast aside.
Assets interest the lawyers, who put fuel to the fires
To boost their fees: they play the blame game.
Money is difficult, but things are only things.
What lasts is the sound of an empty place
That was once a home. It leaves an empty space.

A good parent would do anything, even die for her child,
To live without them nearby is unnaturally hard.
It is Access to and for the Child, only accessible then.
Time is defined, it's limited parenting, restricted thereby
It comes as their right. It's vital to them and it's vital to you.
Time as a Law, is so precious at first, too short and too long.

Access keeps the all pain alive. Love's account is long overdue.

AGAINST THAT COLD *15.5.96*

It was cold, but we smiled, danced
And kissed, said
"Come in let's hold,"
Against that cold.

We laughed and weaved a beautiful
Woollen coat, hung with silver and gold
Against that cold.

You came with so little, so few things,
But so much warmth and laughter and love
Against that cold.

You brought your cares held within you,
And I too told my pain, believed we'd win
Against that cold,

Gladly trusted, shared my all with you.
Two beings each central, centred together
Against that cold

But your care pulled against your heart.
Against that tidal wave I tried to help
Against that cold.

Wrapping your cares around you, you left alone,
Hoping you and I might still be entirely whole
Against that cold.

You took your share and our future in your hands
While I wrapped dark clouds round my loneliness
Against that cold.

We love each other still I know, but a divided
Coat, separate ways? How can we still grow tall
Against that cold?

AIDE MOI - AIDE TOI?

Quasimodo's question "WHY?"
An often final inquiry of God.
As with the lepers, fear fuels prejudice.

A spiteful God who might strike
Down those who are "not like us".
THEY are different, to be punished.

The straight, the well, drew back.
Shouted "Vive la difference."
It's a Gay plague, plague of Gays.

Prejudice, un-Christ like fear
Drew them to shudder at the
Speculations of Armageddon;

Those un-AIDed stand well away.
Band-Aid, Elastoplast to cover it,
Lucozade, Glucosed, sugaring it over.

Help the Aged, NOT those with AIDS,
The young walking wounded away.
Ask not, "Why me?" Judge not, "Why he?"

Be glad you are not one of THEM.
Not a queer, not a junkie, not unlucky.
Give generously Blood Donors,

Bleed for them, drink your tea.
Coins in the collecting box.
And run fast from the third

World of those with HIV.

**Read and written for a fund raising concert by the Rainbow Chorus, Brighton*

ALONE IN HOSPITAL

Alone in hospital bed,
Night time now, snores
From the fortunate ones,

Figures sitting by beds;
Coughs, moans, and
The long empty silences.

Night is the dying time,
Pain time now, fears added
From the imagination.

Figures confined on beds.
Quiet heart beating,
Sobs held deep inside.

The hospital machine
Cranks slowly through
The too-long night.

Staff walk softly by beds,
Torchlight monitoring those,
Pain-filled expressions.

Four hourly Observations
Noted on charts, hooked to
The end of each bed.

A curtained cubicle,
Is it another ended life?
Telling of those

Night Rounds.

ALTRUISM DOESN'T PAY

"I'd love to come, but I haven't any money
Can you lend me any?"

It would cost three pounds to get into the gig.
I would share my money, since I had six pounds.

We each paid our three pounds.
Another friend brought me drink.

The music played too loudly at this fund-raising event for India.
I sipped my beer and watched the friend with my three pounds,

Spend that money on lovely sun pendant
I liked, but could not now afford.
"Shit", I thought, "That's life".

Altruism doesn't pay.

"I'll pay you back tomorrow," my friend smiled and walked away.
Three days later there was no money.
After work, got home to find a pile of junk mail on my doormat.
One was even all screwed up.
As usual, threw them all on the fire, happily watching the flames.

That evening, a phone-call. "Did you get the three pounds?
I hadn't an envelope with me, so I screwed them up in a ball of scrap paper?"

"What is the melting point of a pound coin," I wondered?

The fire had been burning several hours, probably at 800 degrees centigrade.
"Money to burn" I mumbled to myself, as I sifted through the ashes.
"The widow's mite."
I then had to vacuum and dust the whole room.

Altruism doesn't pay.

ANGELS

An Angel came to my bed,
Offered me the chalice of Love.
I drank all its sweetness.

She flew away all too soon, was gone.
Left with silence sharp as flint; with
Words hard as fists against my heart

She had gone, took part of me.
Still loved, was un-loving. Poems
Haunted my nightmare dreams.

I say to all who seek this dream
Of love, "Beware low flying angels."

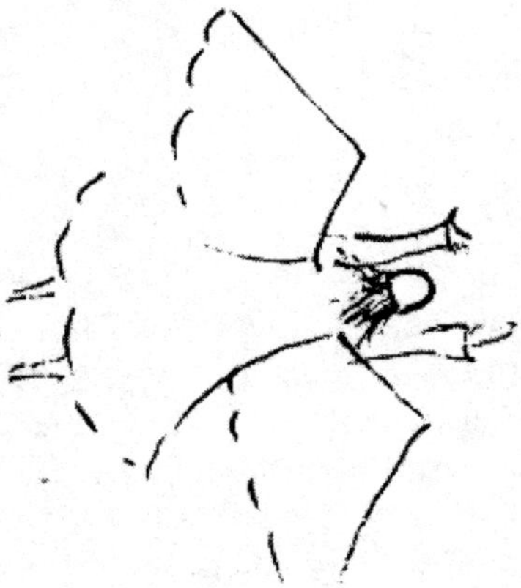

BOTH

A time has come now
To say again

My open hand and true heart
Lie bleeding

Both were held out
Once to you,

Both open, neither wanted
Still offered.

The time has come to
Close the hand and heart.

But what of the Soul still
Bound to you?

AWAKE

Awake, I wind up the clock of my body:
Get up and dress, apply the face:
The mask that I wear to face the world.
Automatically, I drive my automatic automobile
To my automated autumnal work

Cheerfully I chat, I listen, I hurt with others:
Heel, feel their pain and give them hope.
In my nurse's uniform, I am trained to pain:
Dressing, dressings, undressing, bathing, tidying
Toileting, bed making: my strength is always there.

Nursing in Intensive Care, Casualty, Dialysis:
Machines help. Time destroys the waiting
Wounded, waiting round: patiently patients
Attend Clinics, X-ray, Physio, O.T., Maternity:
Real people easily categorised as cases.

Tractioned, suspended, broken bodies, Warded,
Oxygenated, in respiratory distress, classified:
The Nursing Process applied generously,
If time permits. Some stand out as people,
Someone's mother, husband, or child.

I leave the Hospital Ward, uniformed and worn:
Drive home to face the bills, the family, my life:
Children, problems, housework, cleaning, repairs.
Un-uniformed in jeans, I'm still a Nurse.
I re-live patient's pain, their deaths, their hope.

AYERS ROCK

'Illano' the people have always called it,
Illano is their word for permanent.
Like an old red tooth, this sacred rock
Stands proud, part of an older land showing
Through younger flat lands, an island again.

It has been taken from its people, their dreamtimes.
The whites took it two hundred years gone, made it
Their National Park in the eighties, for tourists to visit,
Climb and photograph, just as they take our souls
With their photographs of the people of the rock.

In the Sun this sacred Rock changes colour,
Whilst the light changes with its passage
Through the day. Like ants THEY climb the Rock,
Offending its sacred nature and its people,
Leaving their tracks and rubbish on the ground.

The people are the guardians of the lands,
They walk its dream-lines and song-lines.
It is Whippita, a sacred place; the secret
Cannot be told. The people fear to die if
They say it; it is so powerful to them.

The men of the people were initiated there.
The original people meet now, and tribes
Join to talk to the whites to try to defend it.
There are Land Courts to discuss dream-tracks!
This was a land built in the dreamtimes!

How can you own a dream space?
The People were of the Land.
Whippita took care of them.
We can only be caretakers.

BE PREPARED

★ *Words of the very elderly bar-lady at the Theatre Royal in 1988*

"How do you do?" I ask and think
As I speedily serve that drink
"Do you do well? Didn't I do well?

I look at them all as they all come
At once, at the same time, together:
To the Bar I mean, for Interval drinks.

They want something long, cold and quick
That's my experience of the Theatre.

I have to serve them all, men and women,
Quick and with a smile, ice and all.

It's worse than a gang-bang or an orgy
All this noisy coming at once. I have to
Prepare for it, there is nothing left to chance.

I don't want them to get me into trouble.
I have all my change lined up. I'm ready
For anything! Even Mister Right!"

BESIDE MYSELF

Walking together with other women
In Goddess-land, we discovered so much.
Virginia and Vita might have had to run
To keep up with us, in our laughter and quiet.

We danced, talked, walked and made love.
Almost innocent, we held each other in our hearts.
It was a pure true love, a voyage of self-discovery
And learning each other. Giving was receiving.

Feeling young again, I hoped and believed,
Although when she moved away and even
When she took lovers or sought new magic,
I will not believe we cannot stay friends.

Reading her poems and seeing our photos,
Searching my mind for her voice and image,
Awake or asleep, she is still there beside me,
As real as she will ever be to her new lover.

I am beside myself, for she is not beside me.
Nobody else will do, for I am locked in a love
Which will always be unrequited, now that
She has gone without a backward glance.

Her grievous bodily charm, her clatter of bracelets,
She left, her tongue set free, her face turned away.
I was left with empty panic, not jealousy, stunned,
Bewildered, incomplete, so conscious of the gap.

BITE ON THE BULLET

Is a bullet Catholic or Protestant,
Provisional or Loyal?

Is a bomb Serbian or Croatian?
Dubrovnic does not care.

Is hunger Democratic or Communist?
Ask the Ethiopian.

Is disease Muslim or Hindu?
Bangladesh does not know.

Did the hurricane work for God?
Why does man play God?

When the earthquake came to Mexico,
Did He warn the city of Angels?

Why is a disaster an Act of God?
What a way for a God to act!

Unequal world, where those who
Have-nots have more taken away.

Why does God make no reply?

BLACK BERET

A photo by the canal,
Showed her where to stand,
Naughty wind playing
With skirts and hair.

Stood too near the edge,
The wind whipped off my hat.
It lay, like a black pancake,
Provocatively near, but

Too far for me to reach.
No long stick to hand,
Leaned out, but just
Unable to grab it.

That hat was a statement,
A new me, jaunty, black,
With a scarlet cloth rose,
A diamanté star at the front,

Floppy, friendly,
Fitted loosely,
Lined with silk,
It was warm black velvet.

We watched it float,
Then slowly fill
With green water,
Tip below the surface,

Sink and go from our sight,
Down to the muds below.

BLITZ BABY

★An old lady in a nursing home remembers

"I remember mother -
I have her purse –
After the bomb
They dug it from
The rubble – they never
Identified her body.

I have her purse –
I treasure it –
It had a piece of material –
You see –
It has flowers on –

From some cloth
She wanted to buy –
A medal of Saint Theresa –
I keep them
In this precious purse-

And this was there –
A ha'penny –
This old worn-out
Purse
I treasure it …"

BUSINESS AS USUAL

She opened her eyes, wiped dark night away:
Curtains drawn, light on, she prepared to leave.
She walked to the door, unlocked, unbolted and left:
Open as ever, to go out to meet others, even on time.

Her door opened but could be closed and bolted.
To her lover she even gave a key, but the bolt shot,
Still closed the door to everyone when she wanted.
She needed private space, to close out all others.

Selected visitors were admitted by invitation,
Some regularly, others by chance if convenient.
Rarely hospitable, often lonely, her need for control
Closed the door to the needy, lonely, even to love.

When that door was shut no living creature moved
Or shared her flat. Once she left it became dark,
Without life. Her safe-haven not reached by daylight,
Dark areas, contents secret, only she the key-holder,

She secured secrets, fearful of losing the keys:
Yet no copy was made for another to guard.
Her home was a strongbox, like her heart:
Thoughts shuttered, fearful others may see inside.

CALM

Curved flatness, plateau of water,
Only sea's edge ruffled by
This tide.

Setting Sun sends shards of
Orange light across the water's
Surface,

Split only by the heads of swimmers.
Dog and mistress floating
In gold,

Sweeping limbs barely turning the water,
The brown brine breaking behind their
Two heads,

Bringing a white foam through a calm
Surface.

This gentle swim in the silent August evening,
Land creatures at home in their ancestral medium,
The sea.

Three riders on beautiful brown horses
Bareback, lumber sweetly through
The swell.

No white horses this day,
A surface – no surfers,
A mirror

Sea safe, controlled, no fear
Whilst it rests, in
This calm.

CAT

The cat I live with is black and white.
He's called Oscar, for he's rather wild.
Taken from the litter at six weeks old
This curious cat-child at once explored.
He ate, purred, played and investigated.
Home was his territory, not mine, or the dog's.
After all he could climb curtains, furniture, skirts,
Get inside or under anything; could use the cat flap.

I needed keys, locks held me back. I had to work.
He was lucky, came and went where he pleased
Sleeping when and where and how he wished.
He soon trained me to his likes and dislikes.
His dish was inspected before eating, to approve,
If disapproving, he walked away with a dirty look.
He knew the woman next door, and the people
Over wall were good for a meal or a bed.

If he really wanted food, how loving,
How electric his body became, quivering,
As he rubbed against my legs, dribbling,
His face and eyes expressing such extreme need.
Normally silent, the cat learned dignity early.
He abhorred people watching him do his business,
Was furious if hunting was interrupted or disturbed.
How pained his features, if moved from his sleep.

Always curled in the sunshine, the grate, a lap,
He'd adore cardboard boxes, bowls or bags.
He chased dreams, intimidated the goldfish,
And was utterly unafraid of visiting dogs or cats.
He'd allow a ginger she-cat, a rare creature,
To come into his kitchen, or onto my lap.
Rather she asserted she should come to
Share his food and inspect the residence.

She moved on, but he wasn't troubled,
He knew all the neighbours cats,
How far he and they could go.
He was the benign dictator
Of his home range and lands,
Wild and loving.
I had a position in
His court and heart.

CENTRED

Born elbow first, second daughter, middle child,
A little over a year behind her sister, only in time.

Shared a room when small, but each needed to grow.
Same schools, uniforms, different directions to go.

She was first in sciences, same freckles as her Dad,
Serious, funny, a thinker who smiles even when sad.

Her inner peace showed with her generous sharing
Physically slender, slight, yet strong, dutiful, caring.

A mediator, tried not to take sides, listened, quiet
But thoughtful, kept some things deep in her heart.

She bore three children, each also very different,
With differing needs to be met to help them grow.

Tries to give each equal space, Ellie, Tom and Joe.
See her with her daughter, this very gifted teacher.

She balances all the calls on her too-short time,
Gets tired, but keeps her cool, dependable is fine.

She can swim in or under water, a deep-sea diver.
She was a water baby, a true child of Nature.

Gardens when she can, is an advanced driver.
She is the pillar, who supports those she loves.

She has a kind husband; both work and play hard
She does the garden, helps her man when she can.

Hates the weeding, loves to see things growing.
She spins these plates with grace, keeps it all going,

Leaves her own time to last, not much left for her
After all her duties tries to save us all from falling.

As a mother and a working wife it's her calling

* *To dear Sara 2010*

CHALLENGES

The past disturbs a closed mind,
For we each see a past which
So challenges our present.

Remembering so often is
The real rationale for
How it is now for us.

In many ways it is just that.

The challenge is to remember
The real facts. to find the Truth.

TRUTH

For we mortals truth is no absolute, It must be both objective and subjective.

Things experienced together are remembered apart, having many facets.
Things noticed by one or another may be different, even events shared,
Seen from different places, gives each a separate perspective, an illusion
It will have fascinating angles, decorated, edited, distorted dramatized.

The accuracy of a story or of History is reflected in the character of the person
Interpreting these events. There is no single Truth without context.
It is impossible to get the whole truth about any event or person at any time
We can only draw near to a truth or an understanding.

The cynic might say that the only truth is that we all will die; all lives do end.
Some truth is damaging, our facades are so frail, almost as fragile as truth itself.
Scientific truth is belief based on hypotheses; it gives us terms of reference,
Based on observation, demonstration, experimentation and evaluation.

Religious Truth is based on Faith, with which we may,
Or may not feel comfortable.
Truth is beyond logic, as logic is often beyond truth.
Much truth is a compromise away from untruth.

Easier, lies often feel more comfortable than truth.
The bull at the moment of death in the ring has his moment of truth.

Perhaps that is what death is, our glimpse of the truth?

CHINA

Collecting - the hunt is on,
We go to fairy Castled Arundel's
Market, antique shops and stalls.
We know what we are after.

She's "Gone Chinese".

Little orange brown cups,
Saucers, teapots, bowls,
Bargains, some a bit chipped,
The booty in plastic bags

Placed carefully at our feet.

We drink tea in the genteel
Restaurant garden,
Talk of her collection.
Birds stalk for scraps.

The soft toy she bought for
Another's bed is on my mind.

CITY VISITOR

In Norwich City Car Park a great green cricket
Landed on my arm. She was green as a privet leaf,
So graceful, seeming to carefully count her limbs.

"What's the score cricket?" I asked; but she walked
Up my arm and started carefully to clean her face
With three or four limbs, swaying like a mantis.

We had gone to see the Cathedral, Norman, unique,
Firm against time, its wood and stone carvings,
To taste its history, marvel at its architecture.

Soft-spoken Anglian directions soon got us there,
Against the flow of shoppers, to the main doors.
I remembered my green companion, but then

The cricket jumped off my arm, before we entered.
Perhaps she'd seen it earlier. I had seen the Cathedral
Before, will again, but never a green cricket in a city.

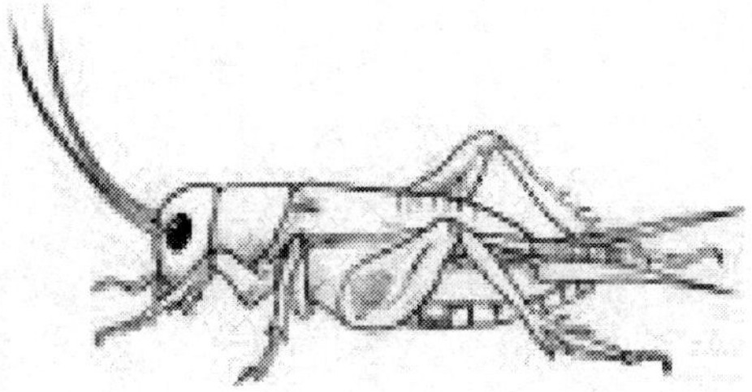

CLONES

He's ambiguous, She's exiguous:
He's ambivalent, She's equivalent
He's androgynous, She's erogenous:
Zones.

He's collectable, She's delectable:
She's incredible, He's just edible:
She's glamorous, He's quite amorous:
Moans

He's masculine, She's feminine:
He's virile, She's fertile:
He's virulent, She's flatulent:
Drones:

He's physical, She's quizzical:
She's stripping, He's flipping
She's ready, He's heady:
Groans

He's mounting, She's counting
He's coming, She's humming:
He's gyrating She's vibrating:
Clones

He's crude, She's nude
He's quaking, She's faking.
He's died, She's lied.
Bones

CLOWNS

See the clown with
Painted face, white.

No falsehood
Behind this mask.

See the pathos, pain,
And the courage,

Join the feel, the
Love in laughter.

The eyes have it
In the dance of life.

Release humanity's
Breath. Feel the

Laughter at our fallings.
Know we can smile

Through our feelings,
But like a clown.

The eyes have it
In the dance of life.

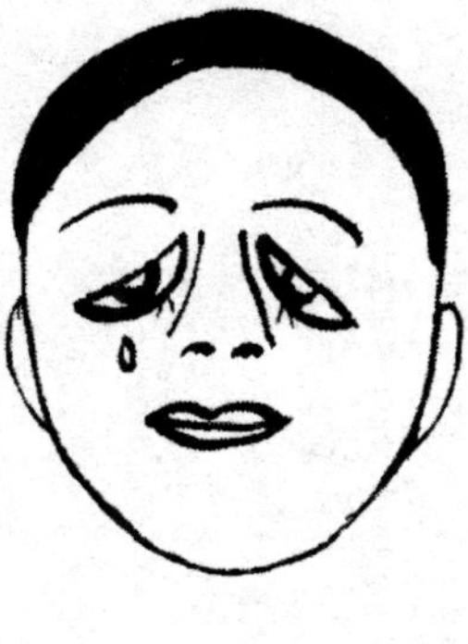

COGITO ERGO SUM

I think of her,
But am not thought of,
Therefore I write of her.

I am, I think,
Still in love with her,
But am not loved

Don't be dismayed
I know it's sad, but
I'm not dissuaded.

I seek word of her,
I am, I think, still
A person worthy of thought

I am not recognised.
Though sad,
I still think kindly of her.

I love, therefore I am
I think, better for this.

After all
Non-cogito, non-ergo sum!

I am not a rock that "is"
But does not think.
It cannot love, nor can it forget.

If I were a rock,
I would "be",
But not think of her.

I might love, and would forget,
And she would forget me still.

I think, therefore I am.
I live, therefore that love still is.

I think, therefore I shall be
And perhaps love lies

In the future for me.

CONFUSIONS

She said:

If you loved me You'd go away
If you loved me You'd let me play

If you loved me You'd understand
If you loved me You'd let go my hand

If you loved me You'd agree to share
If you loved me You'd keep your care

If you loved me You'd show no pain
If you loved me You'd let go again

If you loved me You'd let me go
If you loved me You'd surely know

If you loved me You'd have no needs
If you loved me You'd allow my deeds

If you loved me You'd move on too
If you loved me You'd wait in queue

If you loved me You'd sympathize
If you loved me You'd not criticize

If you loved me You'd let me go
If you loved me You'd wait I know

If you loved me You'd take the blame
If you loved me You'd know the game

If you loved me You'd love yourself
If you loved me You'd still be on the shelf

COUNTRY FOLK

Times moved on and we didn't. Those who moved on moved away,
And newcomers came and took up the old empty ivied cottages,
Restored their comfortable ingle-nooks, kitchens, and bathrooms.
Why, re-plumbed and rewired, it's good as new, but with a view!
In their gardens they grow roses, herbs and hollyhocks. Picture
The double-glazed windowed cottage, centrally heated, mock-tudored,
Secure, respectable, with burglar alarms and pine furniture.
With their gleaming garaged vehicles the Porsche, the Range Rover,
Their green wellies by the door, micro-waving at the lie of all this.

A Victorian, Laura Ashley view of how it really wasn't for country folk.
They weekend; some go for healthy walks, eat health foods, make
Elderberry wine, go through life isolated from rural reality and us.
Part-time villagers, their eyes stay faxed to the ground, tied to the city,
In their inorganic lives, unearthed by city upbringing,
They wipe the good land's soils from their shiny shoes.
Our wellies were black, scratched and caked in old muds.
Our words are slow and few save at home round the fire of
Logs we cut. We never locked our doors, had nothing to steal.
Everything and everyone and all had their place.

Our cottages were crammed with children, not things.
Our world was the village; our ruler was the seasons.
The black dark nights are now illuminated by outside lights,
Lighting nobody's way to anywhere. The dreadful dream
Shadows are gone, like the cobwebs, which filled our
Pre-TV, night-time stories, told around dusty grates,
With ash still aglow; small flickering yellow and blue
Flame filled places in our prehistoric imaginations.
No book or gadgets, our learning our time was spent listening.

Make no mistake; people died in these, our little homes,
Children were born, but many were lost to us.
As tenants or farm-workers there were no mod cons.
Those from the Big House sometimes brought a basket of
Cast-off clothes, a little food, essential charity.
Forelocks were touched. We knew our place.
Encapsulated, they, like us, remain frozen like goldfish
Trapped in the ice of a too shallow winter pond.
It is said that heaven is a place where life resumes,
Then, now, the village is a place where life presumes.

A Bronze Age man has been found frozen in the Alps
Country folk, where then can we find what he thought?

DAD IS DEAD

Dad is dead; it is time to clear his flat:
To go through his private life, in boxes:
To reduce his loneliness to things; in the
Place where he died, we daughters were there.

He was carried from there, as we carry his things:
Reverently, carefully, away from this place of death.
Pictures off walls marked by empty spaces now.
Bed stripped, plastic under-sheet open to air, stale.

Curtains drawn, phone engaged, but no body there.
His books, out of date, once prized yet useless.
His clothes, stained with tobacco burns, for the bin,
Or Oxfam: old pipes, slippers, useless bits and pieces.

Relatives hoping for the same mementoes of him angered:
Disgracing the death, quarrel, discussing the disagreeable
Interpretation of a badly drawn up Will, its complex codicils,
Sad he never realised what was important to each of us.

Old letters written to him from before I was born, kept
In a box, with other papers. Private thoughts to burn or keep.
Old bills and new ones keep coming through the door, to pay.
Read the meters. Cut the gas, water, electricity, and phone.

Photos of people I don't know, unlabelled, in old albums
Of his youth, at university, uniformed in the Royal Artillery,
Poignant glimpses of his time before me. Is there a key in
His life or death to who I am? I have some of his features.

We enjoyed music; he had his 78's, I'm not yet into CD's;
Both old fashioned. The clock has stopped. Dad is dead.
Middle age hits me and I miss him, angry at his expected,
Untimely, untidy passing.

I recall the slime coming from his dead mouth before they
Took him. How cold and unapproachable he was in death.
He understood me a little, and I did him.
I have not cried,,,,, Yet.

DAMAGE LIMITATION

Bomb fell, bombshell! Bomb-blast
Love her, Loves another, love hurts.
Fools paradise, April Fool, trusted.

Secure love, un-secured by truth.
Sinking slowly in a swamp of tears.
Accepted hateful facts, untrue love!

No reminder to them, of that pain.
Yet again ran for a shelter,
The sirens' call.

Blocked the past in concrete,
Moved on to try forgetting.
To walk tall

Tried to secure self-confidence
Before it too was lost at sea, lost
With all hands

Once was true, but dare not trust again
For some time to come. Took time,
Both the enemy and a healing friend.

Grieved with friends, learned laughter again.
The un-true lover lost more than you of truth.
Self-deceived that love was untrue,
Not the lover.

Just a girl.

Do not become one of the faithful dead,
Move on to a new living life, perhaps love.

Rise despite, not because of, the devastation.
This was history,

An old story

Become an architect, build, shore-up
Foundations founded on honesty.

Build well against the blast in the open
Shelter nearby.

DANCING TO A DIFFERENT TUNE

We dance to a Beethoven Quintet,
A Classical Minuet. In stocking feet,
Taped incongruity in the darkening room,
Candlelight's flicker, on plays the music,
Touching us with its mind and melody.

Nervous fingers undo my clothes,
She's never undressed another woman before.
Each forbidden revelation delights.
Breasts touch, sweep across each other,
Nipples erect. It's too soon for each.

We agree a contract. Must not love.
Smiling open eyes search for clues.
"What should I do?" she asks directly.
"It's so easy, do what YOU like".
She likes everything; talks it through.

The delight, sighing sobs, curved movements.
So long leaves it, not going for the jugular,
Teasing through covering clothes, then under.
Stroking thighs, behind knees, under arms, necks,
Even elbows - an exploration of mirrored movements:

Turn taking, again and again, wet before we start.
Gentle fingers deep inside, flickering, stroking,
Probing, holding, rubbing. No mistakes, each takes
And gives a sexual release, startling both again.
Again and again we come. "Come Again," we sing.

Naked on the floor, golden bodies in candlelight.
She's a carer, knows words can be bullets, thinks,
Makes me feel whole and confident.
Not in love, we like each other.
She feels my whole inside outside stress,

Knows to caress.
Oh, what can I do?
Surely she loves it too?

DAUGHTERS

The women lay together, skin against skin,
Nipples touching. naked, alike yet different.
The older plump, strong, tired, felt younger in her arms.

The younger woman, child-like grew wise in her caress.
No power in their lovemaking equality,
Taking turns at the giving and receiving.

Smooth, soft bodies, twinned, cool or hot,
Merging in female scents and senses.
Whole beings joined in this understanding:

Sisters, switching, mother-daughters, lovers:
They played games with each other sometimes.
Children of the Goddess, daughters, equals,

Rebels against tedious
Patriarchal conventions,
But true to themselves.

MERMAIDENS

Into clear blue water they plunge,
Sea pink fish bodies, mermaids awhile,
Cast asunder by stormy worlds,
They lie on the beach, like castaways.

Pale solitudes on the golden burnt sands
Fin-marks and stones upon the shore.
No Man Friday, no rescue ship wanted
No longer amphibians, but girls.

Hot Sun rays melt the illusion – the
Mythological creatures mere mortals
Who swam together in joy that day,
Together, briefly, then walked away.

DAY OUT IN ARUNDEL

January mists over the Arun,
Castle little greyer than the sky,
River mist up the high street,
Antiques invite us inside.

Pub with log fire - 'Black Rabbit,'-
Real ale, while the river runs high.
Few customers this day, by televised
Gulf War and the cold dissuaded.

Bookshop and tea-shop genteelity:
High prices not greatly grudged.
Our Earl Grey in china cups,
In a room with a Venetian ceiling.

Duke in his castle,
Catholics in Cathedral:
The Parish Church divided
By glass, others by class.

A cathedralised place,
Not a city, more
A large village, grown
About a family history.

We walk back to the car,
Un-greyed by this day.

DEFINED BY LOVE

So many women define their worth by being loved or unloved.
A mother assumes she is loved, wanted and valued by her child.
When the baby so needs her, she knows she has a reason.
As the infant grows, the reasons become more complex,
Perhaps that's why mothers often cry at weddings.

A typical wife moves in with her man, allows his person,
His surname, to supersede hers, so she knows she belongs.
A feminist grown stronger may stand more independent,
But she needs her sisters and her fight for justice. Seeking
Equality often brings many to emulate the worst in men.

The lesbian is no loner, she needs to be wanted and loved,
For her it is still a search for security in an insecure world.
It is harder for her with all conventional society's pressures,
Her choices are smaller. Roles still persist. Her partner
May become a "mother" or "daughter" figure, rarely "sister".

Perhaps relationships can only be equal given space:
If we oscillate between roles, so each can feel and be
Wanted, needed, large or small, protecting or nurtured.
A tree alone can stand tall, two together can be
The same height, each grown, given the same light.

Our worth should not be defined by being loved, but
It is rather easier to love ourselves if we are so loved.
The value of our love is more an expression of our own
Worth. In loving securely, sincerely and without condition
We show how strong and weak we are; we know we exist.

Love locked out, we may thrive, the independent woman,
If it is possible to love oneself, one's work, or cause or art,
But something important is missing without that sharing.
We gain by giving and love by living, even live by loving,
But are not entirely defined by being loved.

DESERT HEART

**Adapted from the Psalms*

The land of my love lay lifeless,
This dry, cracked country once rich.
The seed of my love lay suspended
Awaiting love's God's given gift.

In the Fall, Sun's heat was diminished
And drops of life's pure water began.
The tears of joy we both cried then
Grew to torrents of life-giving love.

Dust became soil, seeds soon to buds,
Brought great rare blooms to our land.
I had felt as a stranger within it,
Now knew it again, just as of old.

My mind knew her better than I did myself,
The flower of this love grew so well,
It became a land rich in milk and honey,
Like the Biblical Manna, that desert bloomed.

Behold, a heart which, though young,
Had grown old, weary, revived, survived.
These two hearts were joined with a pure love,
And like the brief desert flowers grew strong.

All that we have to give is love.
No heart in the desert for me.
The flowers will still
Bloom on that land.

A time that we share,
Is a time that is rare,
Brief blooming desert
Can and will turn fair.

DIFFERENT

A mermaid swam in the deepest deep
Having felt the sunrise in her heart.

Cold rough water soothed her soul,
Passion's fire lost in deep dismay:

Remembering a land-mortal's fingers
Once stroked her hair. Both could swim,

Each belonged in different worlds,
Under water the other needed air.

Mermaid could not walk without her help,
Could not run: The other could swim,

But in deep oceans she could not breathe.
Eternal love lost in a moment, like the Unicorn.

The mermaid saw her run along the shore, away,
Where they once held each other, a way from love.

A way she could not take. Waited for her to turn,
Return; look back to see, only to say farewell.

DIFFERENT EYES

Embraced by the Euphrates and Tigris lies Mesopotamia,
Whence the arts of civilisation were brought.
At Edrido was the Garden of Eden, all was harmony.
A ziggurat to Inana marks its religious centre.
This, the stepped pyramid, is a remembered form,
A shape seen from Egypt to Peru and Mexico.
Were they of the same people, or are we all
The same? Our minds holding primal memories,
Dream shapes, Powerful, magical geometry?

Round the city lay a six-mile circuit of walls,
Stood fifty feet high - the height of ten men.
Were there giants then? Why do we still feel small?
Now it has all gone from these Euphrates planes,
Over exploitation, an explosion of population,
Then starvation, Eden worked out by soil erosion.
Like us, they gave nothing back to their mother
The earth, which they plundered, paradise ended.
This Eden, gone now, a fragile paradise lost.

How many miles to Edrido? It is our backyard.
They left us Alcohol, a Mesopotamian word, and escape.
Their city ended in the third century after Christ,
Emptied after five millennia of continuous habitation.
On a wall in the abandoned, deserted, dusty city is written,
"The future is certain whilst the past is imponderable".
They knew mothers and daughters look at the world with
The same eyes, we look at the same world with different eyes.
Open your eyes to Edrido. Its present reflects our future.

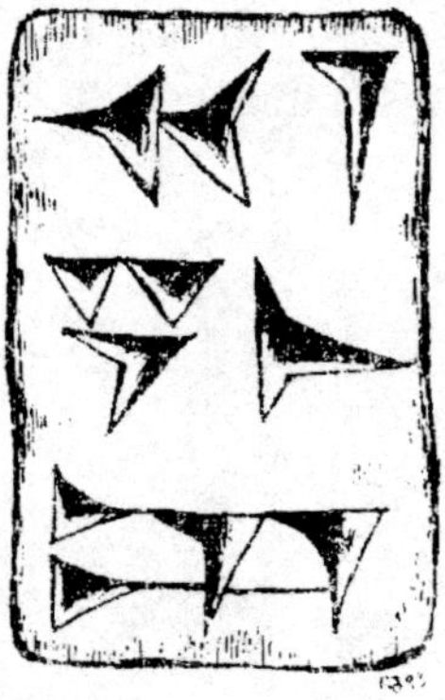

DISORDERLY HOUSE

I keep a disorderly house.

It is chaotic, things all over the place.
Full of people, of objects, and of pets.

As an earth mother I seem to gather
This array of comforts and problems.

I'm always there. When I'm there
I worry; when I'm away I worry.

Why worry, I wonder? At least
I know I'm alive, I suppose.

Perhaps I should do less, become a hermit,
Throw out unused things, say NO sometimes.

But then it would not be the same for me,
I'm used to these things, you see.

There is so much beauty in others, in Nature,
In caring, in sharing and in living.

There is no time to worry about money,
About health, about tomorrow:

Let's get through today, and learn to
Bend with the wind; laugh with the rest,

Especially at myself, and to go on
Just believing and loving for the best.

DO YOU UNDERSTAND

The sense of disorder and the completion in love?

The ache when you want to hold her, but she's too tired,

The animal pleasure of the scent of her juices on your fingers,

The peace as you lie together, excitement at kissing, holding,

The quickened heart at her smile, laughter, being together,

The sound of her voice, pleasure at talking, in listening,

The safety in a plan shared, challenge of building, learning,

The sadness at critical difference, despair in loss and leaving,

The excitement in mutual interests, sharing, being together,

The dismay in being last in line, the delight in being first,

The support in being needed, vulnerability in wanting to help,

The exquisite sense of equality and yet genuine admiration,

The harmony with oneself and her, knowing and feeling together,

The bridge between souls, the eternal space twixt one another,

The mystery of her mind and emotions, familiar but surprising,

The genuine joy she brought to my life?

So what does,

Or did,

Pain ever matter?

DOWNLAND SUNSET

North facing scarps dip to seaward, low Wealden skyline below sea's horizon,
Seen from the Dyke, its sheer V sided cleft winding into the chalk massif.
Only the Devil could have built it to flood the dark-Weald below.
Symbolic myth to explain Satan stopped mid-dig by a cock's crow.

This most atypical valley cut along a fault line, caused as the African Plate
Collided with Europe, Post-Cretaceous, that continent moves inexorably,
Bulging the Wealden anticline, cut in two now by the older marshy soft
Wealden clays and hard sands, exposed by Ice Ages, to rain and rivers' erosion.

These lands lay, a patchwork of fields, hedgerows, farms, villages and roads.
The Greensand ridges East-West, punctuate the Gault and Weald Clays.
North Downs face south in the distance, mirror their Southern sisters.
Grey mist monochromes the lowlands, now slowly sweeps up the rivers,

Moving South like a cloak to welcome the night. No longer a proud Ring,
Chanctonbury Scrub marks the far edge of the pale, visible scarp to the West.
Behind and to its left an orange orb sinks quickly on this October glomin,
Illuminating the undersides of schools of whale-like cumulus, drifting east.

A cold wind sails these apricot-tinted grey cloud masses, standing seemingly
More solid than the once iridescent land against the sky. The Sun deepens to
Gore-red, sinks, grows larger: This haloed orb, drips blood hues and sends
Celestial shafts of light with glorious golden power to dance on the sea and
Spotlights areas of land.

The air chills as radiant heat is withdrawn and the mist closes on the grey-green
Southdown land. Village lights, car headlights, a single aircraft, out from Gatwick,
Its green and red wing lights, reveal people and their movements The Dark Age
People were fearful of the Weald Forest and of its night's demons.

The birds are silent now and night is upon us: Premature as autumn nights
So often can be. A vague translucent crescent-moon stands to the south,
Low in the heavens. Light years away, the sleepy stars blink into view,
Their brightness polluted by our electric city lights. Star scapes are rare.

No Milky Way, no shooting stars this night, no comet to bring us awful dread.
It is moon-time now, a time to prepare for Winter Solstice, night demons,
Bonfires, overcoats, Wassail songs, bonfires and cider promised ahead.
A final, flat, crimson slither is the sun's last nightlight, goodnight,
And farewell on that day.

DRAGON FLY

Preserved in amber was the dragonfly:
She was reached by careful probing.
Cells taken from the preserved body
Were implanted in gel, then treated
And inserted in modern dragonfly eggs.

The fertile eggs hatched, bio-engineered
Back from extinction.
The larvae grew,
And began
To feed
On
Us

DRIFTWOOD

Driftwood washed, wet still,
On to the pebbled beach;
Fashioned by the tides
And Torredo Worms,
Which bored
Holes into it.

Its beauty unmatched,
This natural form
Released an idea
In my imagination,
A remembrance of a
Shape I knew.

Varnished and polished
Washed and dried,
Put carefully in place,
This chance object

Now become art.

DUCK!

"Duck!" "Watch out!" Friends called.
I felt the arrow before I could see it,

On a true flight to my open heart.
I stared into the pool of my lover's eyes,
Weary from defending her from
Her own fears,
I had my own.

I turned my back to see whether
An arrow had been fired.
Then her blade struck my spine.
She watched
Me bleed alone.

I was gagged,
"You are not to talk, even quietly,
You might say too much",
She spoke her calm words.

I believed our love was written in
Parchment words and proclaimed
By the rings we wore,
They had no meaning.
Trust died in me.

My January soul was filled with
Stone grey cement.
I had tried to be her champion.

Alone now, was grown
Weary and needed rest.

Well, I could rest now.

HEELS OVER HEAD

I am head over heels,
But feel heels over head.

Upside-down, my Downside's up.
Heels over head, it's Head down,

Headache, Heartache.

She's going, but thinks nothing
Will change. But loss is change.

Partings separate, in the hair,
Of the waves, the waves goodbye.

It's not the goodbye of,
"I'll see you later".

Lips and fingers touching,
My hand seeks hers,

It's not there.

Once smiling-lips closed,
Faced now by a frown.

My eyes see spring
Through the tears.

She is my left,
She was my right:
Still is.

But I'm falling over now.

EELS

It's eels we're after.
The mad pub woman glares.
We have maggots and ham
To lure them from between
The cluster of boats.

"Hope you get a bite".
The pink blue evening light
Plays with circles on golden
Flat green waters surface.
Rods reflections curve.

"Let's get a drink".
We sip brandy in the bar
Bucket of eels writhing
In the boot of the car:
Eel menus on our mind.

ELEPHANTS

They came across the bones of one of their kind, bleached
White in the sun, stark against ochre African soil.
It was hot. Their great ears flapped; frowned furrows
Formed along their trunks and foreheads and
Round their sad brown eyes.

Matriarchs, daughters and sons inspected and sniffed.
He was not of their tribe, this old bull elephant,
Who had died alone. No poacher had stolen his
Ivory, bleached white as in life.

A young female lifted his tusk to her mouth,
Held tenderly, delicately, in pity for one of her kind.
Great grey feet nudged the dead bones:
Trunks touched and gently lifted,
In dismembering, remembering,
This old dead bull.

Each bone gently carried into the bush, to be lost or hidden.
Even calves dragged rib bones away from this place of death.
He had spread his seed, and they
Distributed his bones.

Two young females pulled the skull,
Trunks through eye sockets, into a gully:
Distractedly they searched for more of him.
Then, slowly, they left,
Mother's trunks
Shielding the young.

FOOTPATHS

Take comfort in the landscape,
Forget the lost hedgerows.

See the reality of modern farming,
The farm factory landscape.
Go to the farm shop, selling
Imported apples, inflated priced
Dirty vegetables, gone organic.

Park near the slurry pile,
Breathe the fouled air.
Feel the force of the land,
The economic force.

Animals, even butterflies, are
Farmed, as you perhaps are
Fooled into believing you have
Not lost your links with the soil.

Get real mud on your boots.

Upland farmers have their lowland tourists.
The Countryside's now a theme park, its
Dry-stone walls, stonewall you into paying
More to keep uneconomic land rich.

Rich landowners still grow fat,
Whilst you live in rented plots.
Why, the whole countryside's a car park.
Wind your Downland ways,

Walk the Pennine pilgrimage.
Wainwright is dead, a footpath a political
Act; a statement; that urban man
Can plod the ways of his forefathers.

The rural idyll still pays the ways
Of the idle rich. Those less fortunate
Still pay to glimpse how others live.
Farmers work the land, deserve to live well.

Others walk on, searching for footholds.

FOR THE LAST TIME

For the last time I say, "This is for the last time".
Time heals, passes so quickly if happy, so slowly, if sad.
Lovers glimpse Eternity beyond the confines of the finite,
Love lost, we linger in timing our days, and courting our end,
Running through life, away from where we want to be,
Yet dare not, can't be, in the arms of she who went away.

The pendulum clock clicks away our seconds;
Our life swings from happy to sad, and back,
But in unrequited seconds hours pass, frozen, timeless agony.
We may reject love to protect ourselves from that pain,
Build iron walls about our hearts, but human, they beat on,
Until their time's end, and the motion stops.

Stars, sun, earth, moon, all orbits creating our time,
Days, nights, hours, moonlight, starlight and sun,
The stars are always above; we can't see them for the sun,
The moon floods the night, but may be covered by cloud,
Mist, tears and grief cover our sight from that light,
Fossilised in self-pity, we can see no way beyond death.

The optimist turns the clock forward, set ahead
She seeks astrological, those tarot created images,
Of good times to come, or she puts the clock back,
Under a glass jar, she is trapped, observed by a cold God.
If God gave us love, hope and faith, Then that faith
Enables us to grasp the hopeless, to believe again.

With strong love in us perhaps we grow near to
God, who, we are told, forgives and loves all,
Who lived on Earth, and rose from the dead.
God could do that; can love rise again for all of us?
Hope makes us hopeless, unrealistic in a real world,
Where happiness is timed. Those we love die, or go away.

How can we turn our backs on love?
Is it really possible to hate and destroy each other?
How far from perfection have we drifted?
We deceive ourselves if we believe we can
Hurt others without gravely injuring ourselves.
Yes, love does conquer time, as time defeats our love.

FOSSIL*

The rock cracked to reveal
A shape, that of a life-form
Paralysed in stone, petrified,
A time-capsuled revelation
Of a now extinct species.

It was a skull, strangely round,
Still white, but with yellow iron-stain,
Or some other chemical, in parts.
Where eyes once stared, blank
Grey mudstone filled the sockets.

Some teeth remained in the upper jaw.
The lower jaw was misshapen,
But held regular white teeth.
There were some artefacts present
In these chaotic dangerous deposits.

We believe it to be an almost intelligent
Life-form, some sort of humanoid.
It was very radioactive, and the
Cobalt half-life-decay placed it at
Around the twenty-first century.

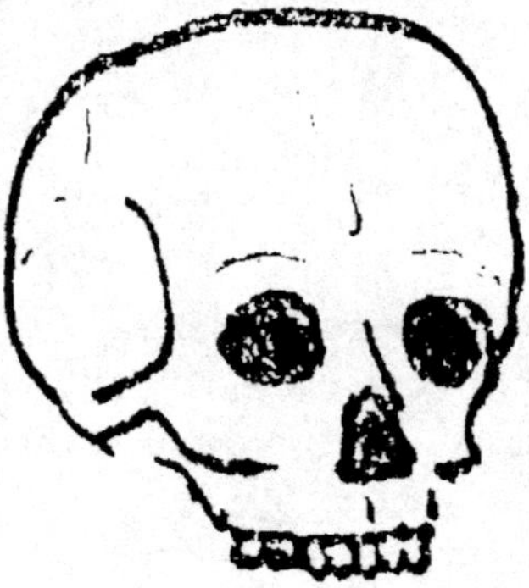

* *The Oxford Museum of Natural History had a display of Geologic Periods, going from Precambrian all the way to Pliocene, Pleistocene then "Pyrocene". A post-nuclear world war display, with melted artefacts and traces of an extinct species… us. Makes you think!*

GAGOUJOU LANDS

Forty thousand years continuity is
Ending, Dreamtime has come:
The living have lost their heritage.
Three old men remain, custodians,
Keepers of the Sacred Ceremonies;
Workers of the art-prayers
Hand-stencilled signatures,
Their sign of immortality.

Sacred places, burial rites, walkabouts,
Song cycles of creator beings,
Remembered and spoken.
Paintings of Ancestral animals,
Songs to the Australian Desert.
No knowledge is written down.
It survives in them alone,
And is spoken to unbelievers.

These, custodians of the land know,
Better than we, they came at once mortal
And sacred, natural and supernatural.
Their monument is harmony with nature.
What man owns changes, it scars the land.
No animal, no plant, no man is safe.
In the beginning of the Dream-Time, long ago,
Inuanju showed the Gagoujou people
What to do.

He focused the life force.
Now He lives in a great rock.
Could even He be snatched by the
Great Sea Eagle,
Back to Dream-Time,
Far Away
From
His People?

RGJ'91

GO FEARLESS

Our lives are a chain of moments,
If we let them go then what is left?
Real experiences demand all the senses.

Nothing more than love concentrates
Them, save perhaps
The act of death

We risk all in loving, but go, fearless
Towards the joy and the ultimate
End of that love.

To love another in powerful litanies
Against the monotonies of a solitary life
We live briefly,
Like a shooting star

Not to love, even impossibly, is not
To be fully alive.

Injured by love it is easy to retreat,
To tearfully blame oneself or her:

But the fact is there is no
Eternal Flame, burning for
The Unknown Lover.

Monuments of poems,
Symphonies of sound,
Words and music,

Art and scents so well
Recall that sixth
Sense of madness
We call love

GOLDEN JUNE

Topless in June sunshine,
Lovers snug on a rug,

Golden wine, warm bodies,
The poem of her breasts.

Notebook open, her recorded
Recollections of the surreal

Fearful reality taking place,
The push for shared pain.

Minds engage the problem,
As though it could be solved,

By understanding alone.
We are frightened children.

Comfort in each other's arms,
Dreamy kisses dispel despair,

Are more real than blame,
More relevant than before.

Driving the one she needs away,
Forgetting she still gives so much.

But who could not delight
At this woman in her prime?

So here's a space for us,
A still moment of magic,

A memory for us to store,
A golden time in my soul.

HEALING HANDS

I have hands that heal. They heal others, that is.
I lay them, with my words and my love, on the hurt
Of others.

Touching their hurt, I feel their pain and try to earth it.
Earth mother them, too much perhaps, for sometimes I
Grow weary.

In my time of pain I find I cannot heal myself alone.
I extend my arms round tree trunks, seek the help
Of others'

Healing hands, touching others with my own pain is a
Task far more difficult for me to do, rather than to
Share theirs.

My hands are strong, wide palmed, long fingered even
Delicate, often clumsy, rarely cold, nails too long for
A nurse.

Placed in another hand, on another hurt, I know they help.
Some hands; hand some to me, sometimes, for weary, I may
Hurt too.

HOLD ON LOVE

Who'll look away first sweetheart,
As golden leaves fall
Towards winter?

A grey cloud obscures our love,
Closer now, in distance.
The music of solitude drifts
Through my days: never alone,
Yet exigent pain filling almost,
That great gap in my life.
Is it Love on hold?

Imprudent dreams and
Needs impinging on my
Oneness and my half-ness.
Like the growth of
An uprooted plant,
Without sunlight,
I will wither.

I love to look at you,
But see you leaving,
To hold you,
The scent of your body,
The taste of your tongue,
To hear you speak
Your gentle words.

I don't want transience.
I'm for the infinite.
I tasted the forbidden apple
And found it good.
Life is become marginal.
Loss is all I know,
Without you near me

HOT WATER BOTTLE

No chance to say goodbye,
She left so slowly that I never
Saw her move.

My heart stood fast, betrayed loves
Dreams seen in her eyes were
For Another.

Transiting from one set of arms
To another is something she
Knew well.

Sometimes in my minds eye,
Though gone and imperfect, she
Is still there.

I loved her, with an open heart.
The greatest gift, I could offer
Was given,

Only, too late I knew she'd found
Another prize.

Dream eyes turned to where she lay
Beside me, opened eyes to a tear
Filled pillow.

Cold water bottle in my bed.
Sleep-time's filled with dread.
Twixt crisp sheets, corpse like,
I lie alone in shawl and bed-socks.
Years have gone.

Lucky indeed is my next love,
Fidelity is always found in me.
Loss of trust, the casualty
Of our together-times.

What sanguine emptiness
Weighs heavily for the Love-Lost.

The more empty a heart
The heavier it feels

Never say Goodbye,
Never saw me cry.

HOVE

Ave Hova! Floreat Hova!
Peek Performance!
I trod in it.

Hove, the town of distinction!
Retire to the town of extinction.

Newhaven for the Continent;
Hove for the incontinent.

Brighton is right on
B. right on.

A pier and a half.
A pierette.

Chain Pier gone
Chain pulled on another.

Just the Palace,
The Royal Peer.

Pavilion, Royal Palace,
Out of its blue plastic box*,

A town like the Palace
Blue plastic.

Celebrate the Festival,
In chip buttied Regency
Splendour.

Dirty weekends in one
Peaks and troughs in the other.

Brighton rocks,
But Hove Actually rolls.

Joined, this unlikely couple
Share the same beach pollution.

Borough of
Hove

BRIGHTON
BOROUGH COUNCIL

* *For several years during restoration the Royal Pavilion, Prinny's Palace was encased in blue plastic sheeting. Sadly the West (half) Pier is only a mangled skeleton now.*

HURRICANE '87

Chanctonbury Ring; village unimportant below the Downland scarp,
High on the hill lay watching the Weald a bear-shaped crouch of black,
Monumental. Trees clustered within that Ring are seen from afar.
It stood timeless, permanent, wild, within man-made embankments.

That wind blew trees, trunks and branches, scattered like dominoes
From the south, each taking northerly sisters or spars as they fell.
They lay parallel, like ranks of a fallen army. High as three men their
Roots turned up like the boots of the dead, opening that sacred ground.

Soil trapped, tangled in roots, chalk revealed: old stones, scrapers,
Boiling stones, broken Roman tiles, rubbish, rough flints, fossils,
And mountains of dead wood. Damaged beyond repair in our time;
The Ring still stood, skeletal, old remembered trees gone forever.

We imagined the trees used to be the old Roman stockade, but they were
Planted by a Rector two hundred years before, but became timeless,
These trees and their young, thrived, formed a copse, to add mystery
To this already magical site, a haunt of lovers of it and of each other.

Within the ring are ghosts, Mesolithic, Druidic and Mithras temple sites,
They conflict, together with Christianity, and with older darker forces.
A place to celebrate May Day, to watch the sun rise, to dance, to walk,
To picnic, for girls to laugh, to see from afar, to visit. A landmark.

A secret place to hold onto; yet share with others in trust; a Ring
Where we hear the wind gently rustle leaves and branches.
A place we danced and kissed, other lovers initialled in wood,
So many trees gone, these old friends and you, so new in the Ring.

I'LL RACE YOU

"Come along, I'll race you"
"But you will always win!"

"Come along, I'll pace you"
"But how did this begin!"

"Come along, I'll face you"
"I'm sure it is no sin!"

"Come along, I'll know you"
"Before it is too late."

"Come along, I'll show you"
"I'm sure it must be fate"

"Come along, I'll LOVE you"
"It's time to set the date!"

I'VE HEARD IT SAID

I've heard it said that
We grow through suffering,
Perhaps that's why I'm fat.

Yet the plump have large
Personalities in general;
And empty hearts in particular.

We are cuddly and laugh a lot,
At ourselves, not at underdogs
For we are the underdogs

In a world of slim credibility.

In Arabia a plump woman is
Considered beautiful, but who
Likes sheiks, camels, and sand?

NO! Chocolate is more reliable.

I WET MYSELF

I wet myself the other day.
It just happened.

I was washing the dishes
And it just happened,
All down my legs.

I must learn not to leave
Saucepans full of water
At an angle!

IN JAPAN

In Japan they can not properly pronounce their "**L**"'**s,**
So they don't have the tedium of General e**L**ections,
In their general e**R**ections they boast of their amazing
Erection promises and manifestos.

The streets have hoardings where each party proclaims
That its erection is vital for the good of the nation.
We all know how little will be the satisfaction of the
People once the erection is over.

Of course once erected the promise is soon lost, and the
Post erection debate begins. Firm action was promised, but
All the effort of the erection campaign is seen
As the disappointment it really was.

The head of the party will of course be the Prime Minister
Erect, and once erected he will lead the mass debate against
The opposition, and waste energy pointing a finger at them;
Unless of course it is a hung parliament.

Clearly Japanese erections are as disappointing as those in
Eng**r**and. Indeed world wide there is nothing but let down,
In many countries they don't have erections. Just a man in
Charge. I suppose that is even worse.

Perhaps if women ruled the world there would be just votes
For women, I would cheerfully vote then, there would be no
Erection lies, and the women would know not to hope too much
From any erection, general or otherwise.

IN MODERATION

Oh to smoke again, to eat white bread:
Not to fear critics
For liking meat.

Or to be slim, thin, not to need diets.
To be the image
The media give.

Or to be fat-happy, plump a good feature!
Yes, to be desired
For being me.

For sugar in tea, yes! – White bread at that!
The chip butties!
Enjoying meals!

To be like elders, to ignore the gloomy!
For food fads kill
Our simple pleasures.

To hear stress is relieved by smoking.
It's good for you!
Relax king-sized!

Government Health Warnings applied
To health-food shops,
And bran taxed.

Ban the pulses, ban the additives!
Good food and smoke
In moderation's fine!

I hope.

IN THE FLAT LANDS

In the flat lands lies a city
Of dreams, where women dance
To the music of their laughter.

Canals reflect the sunshine and the
Moon light electric dream-scapes.

I met her at the disco.
We danced and she smiled.

A swan settled in the Herren-Canal,
Perhaps to fly to England later.

Dutch bells rang out,
And her gentle, musical voice,
Said "Goededag".

LIKE CHILDREN

I first saw her sitting by the bar.
Music played at the women's-disco.

She sat alone, smiling,
But looked vulnerable.

I too felt nervous, but
Went to talk with her.

She smiled sweetly,
We drank a Bessenjenever.

Later we danced.

Her body felt small and warm.
We drank a cup of tea

In her apartment.
We lay on the floor

And listened to Mozart,
Curled together, quietly.

Later slept gently,
Like children

INCOMPATIBILITY
⋆ *Some computer SMART speak*

I speak **Smart,**
He speaks **Word Perfect**.
We cannot **Interface.**
We are not **Compatible.**
His **floppy**'s too little,
He doesn't have a **hard disc**.
Our **Databases** are different.
I don't like his **Spreadsheet**.

He tells me of his **megabytes**,
And says he has more **memory**.
He's **laser printing** himself,
But I **dot matrix** myself away.
He uses **Bold,** I press **Escape.**
He tries **Repeat**, I move **Page on**.
We definitely do not **Interface**,
So I quickly erase his **Memory.**

I'll **Write.** We do not **Compute,**
I tried to **Underscore** the problems,
To **Reformat** our **Spacing, Send**
New **Perimeters, Execute** his **Commands**.
There's nothing to **Save.**
He cannot **Justify** this **Load**.
Move, not **Merge, Replace** him.
Unload this **Ruler** of my **Time**.

I tried to keep **Tabs** on him,
But I must **Change type**.
Goto Look in my **Directory**
Replace him. **Search** my **Index.**
I will **Autohelp** myself,
Undelete my own concerns.
Find a new **Name, Split, Zoom**
Far from this man from **Graphics.**

It's time to **Draw** to a **Close.**
My **Equipment** is still **Indented**
By his **Display.** I could **Execute** him!
I have no **Confidence** in him.
As a **Footnote** I can say
He did **Insert** some joy to my
Visible borders, but **Left** me
To **File** and **Paint Lists** of

Never agains.

INTERFLORA SOME GUILTY GIFTS

I forgave my mother – mother's day flowers.
I dislike feast days – an Easter bouquet.
I slept with another – flowers for my wife.
I forgot my lover – chocolates and flowers.
I will sleep with you – flowers as a bribe.
I put you in an old-folks home – flowers to go by the bed.
I forgot your birthday – flowers to amend.
I survived – a wreath was sent
I left it too late – flowers made it OK

I chose a printed label to say sincerely that I forgot.

I forgot you alive, sent flowers to the funeral.

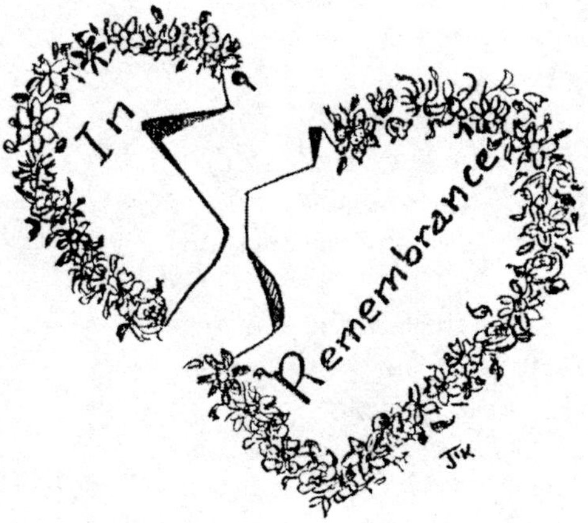

IT SEEMS

It seems free will has a sweet tooth
It seems that choice is often hard
It seems we go slow-time for sad
It seems that it is quick-time for glad

It seems time is stacked against us
It seems we never have enough time
It seems there might be time in the end
It seems there might be an end of time

It seems we are mortal and limited
It seems we are timeless, immortal
It seems work and sleep take up too much time
It seems work and sleep are both good

It seems both needs deprive us of "Our Time"
It seems we need both of them
It seems we need to be loved and to love
It seems love is a dangerous thing

It seems friends are more reliable than family
It seems blood can be thicker than water
It seems we need time to grow and pain to go
It seems working through pain makes us grow

It seems there might be time in the end
It seems there might be an end of time
It seems it's good to take the lead
It seems it is sometimes easier to follow

It seems that no choice is easier than choosing
It seems taking time to work through sadness is best
It seems we must use our time wisely
It seems we always should take our time

It seems love is a wonderful feeling
It seems pain stunts us, who wants it?
It seems life is a circle dance, going in a direction,
Whilst looking back and forward, or so it seems

IT STRIKES ME

Church clock strikes.
Started on strike myself
Two years ago.
A strike while
The iron was hot.
The foundry closed down.
Gone fishing.
Fish strikes.
I play him.
It's no game.
Out of work.
I strike and
The wife strikes me.
Strike a match.
I need a light.
A light at the end
Of this tunnel.
Too old at 55.
Too 55,
Two 55.
Strikes me too old
For the labour exchange
Strike up the band.
Abandon hope.
Strikes a chord.
Hope springs,
Another spring
Out of work,
Out of mind
Out of sight.
Out of it.
Line broke.
I'm broke.
I'm skilled.
I'm stricken,
It strikes me.

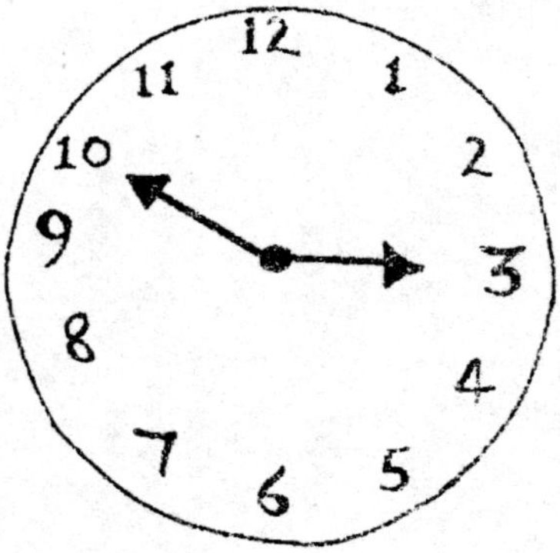

IT WAS HARD

My fingers lifted it to my lips.
It was hard yet soft,
Smelt forbidden, dreadful yet inviting.
It was straight and long.

He said he wanted me to do it …
I placed the end in my mouth,
Holding it between my right thumb
And forefinger.

My hand shook, my pulse quickened.
I withdrew it, touched the end with
My tongue tasted it.
I wanted to take it in
As I once used to do.

Held securely in my mouth
I sucked at it,
As he lit the filter tip.

God, it was good to have
A cigarette again …

JUDEN DES GHETOSKI ...
***Words from a Diary Jan. 17th. 1945**

Rifle butts against the door.
THEY have come.
"Go to the right",
THEY shout. I go there.
Other people come but
They are not my parents.

First snow, twelve noon. Cold.
It's easier to fill an empty stomach
Than an empty stove.
The ghetto is dirty white
Like the frozen dead. Rumours
About what happened to the children.

We pray for a miracle.
Only a miracle can save us.
Why are we in this place?
Will there ever be a tomorrow?
There is nowhere like this anywhere!
Come to save us.
We only want to live.

There is no justice left in the world,
Less in the Ghetto.
The Jewish police stay fat.
How we hate them,
More than the Germans.
Yet nobody fights back.
Like them we are the
Servants of the authorities.
They are only obeying orders.

At last we see deliverance; we are to go.
The trains will take us from the ghetto.
We are to be moved from this hell.
Eighty to a wagon. Some died. Our lives,
Our hopes were shattered.
God had deserted His Chosen.
Delivery came at a place called Auchwitz.

KEEP NORMAN MONKS

Castle Acre, its shelled empty Norman keep,
Thickest of broken walls, grassed slopes,
On which wild cabbage grows purple, erect
Against their grassed steepness, penetrated
With ease and with our Heritage cards.

A walk round the Priory, its Cluniac cloistered
Foreign skeleton, gutted as a stone quarry by
Locals over the centuries, easier to plunder
For good stone, than the ground of the village.

Decorated Norman arches amaze us by remaining
Intact against nine centuries of local lads and
Weather. A house gleaned from the Priors rooms:
Tudor, steadfast, still glazed, haunted and empty.

Smell of old wood, rotting timbers, fungied stone.
Cold fireplace great and open to bird droppings.
Bats transept the ruined skeletal priory church.
Monks' chants no longer heard save in headphones.

No visible graveyard, few artefacts, not a cross
To see. Years of worship gone in this lovely ruin.
High church in a Norfolk sky, open roofed to rain.
Not much comfort now in these deconsecrated acres.

K.I.A.

★ *Written soon after the First Gulf War.*

K.I.A.by Triple A, my brother in death, the invader,
Taken now, home to his land. this American crusader.
Was it a withdrawal, or surrender?
Our land was won.

We'd strafed men like him, young men, like me, With triple A.
They saw our column, Republican Guard,
Nose to tail, along the straight road to Holy Baghdad.

We had heard the call to arms, the Jihad,
Saddam's police were watching my family.
The Ba'ath Party was not of my choice.

I was volunteered with my brothers to defend our Faith,
Our homeland, our women and way of life.
I had no power, just children and my young wife.

Power and oil were what mattered, not little men like me.
Our President was still safe, Damn-sad, was no Mahdi,
Not Holy but wholly war, see the dead children by the road.

Now I lie an "E.K.I.A". Was I his enemy? You see
Not a person, a statistic, the alphabet hides the man.
Westerners like to use initials as a shorthand for a life.

This sand tastes just the same as the sand from home.
Like the POW's, I'm out of the Conflict Zone.
Some GI's were respectful as they covered me with the bunker sand.

KOSOVO

* *A nightmare during the Bosnian War*

I reached the shelled out swimming pool rubble.
A grey dust and sickly sweet blood's stench filled
My nostrils. Guns rattled around us - my helmet was gone.
We were told there were wounded freedom fighters inside.

I reached the objective first - ran for cover.
The others were pinned down by the bombardment.
I had a blue case of drugs for them on my back.
Cut and bruised, my fear had caused me to wet myself.

But I had to help, to see what I could do.
In the rubble there was a gap, a view of inside.
Amazed, I saw there was still water in the pool,
Or something like water, which my disbelieving eyes saw.

The torch beam lit a brown-pink porridge of blood, faeces
And vomit, in which floated a mangle of twisted corpses.
Perhaps sixty, perhaps them all, all civilians.
Women, children, the old, babies, floating like a raft

Of rotting leaves on a pool's stagnant waters, bits of people,
An upturned hand reached through the floating horror.
Perhaps someone was still alive in this dead soup:
A man cried "There's no room in here, we're all dead".

But I was pulled through the gap by another man with
An old Luger in his hand

"Have you come to fight, we need fighters
"No, to help. I'm a nurse".
"Where are you from?"

"United Nations"
"United What?"

LA RONDE

The Merry-go-round covers some ground,
It turns and returns and goes round and around.
The musical horses rock up and rock down,
The lovers moved nowhere in circles.

Woman with man, then with woman again;
She turns and returns and goes round and around.
The whimsical lovers rock up and rock down,
Change partners again in this circle.

Lose sight of all friends; lose sight of all care;
You turn and return and go round and around.
The love that you give is the love that you'll get,
Learn nothing, and live life all in circles.

So strike up the band, and play the old tune.
Time to return and go round and around.
The care that you give is the care that you'll get,
The faithful left dancing in circles.

Cheat yet again, yes dish out the pain.
Turn and return and go round and around.
The man you deceive, the man you will leave
While true love lies dying in circles.

Tell him it's kinder; don't tell him, it's not;
Turn and return and go round and around.

"It's only a phase, please excuse me".
Unsure, as we dance, all in circles

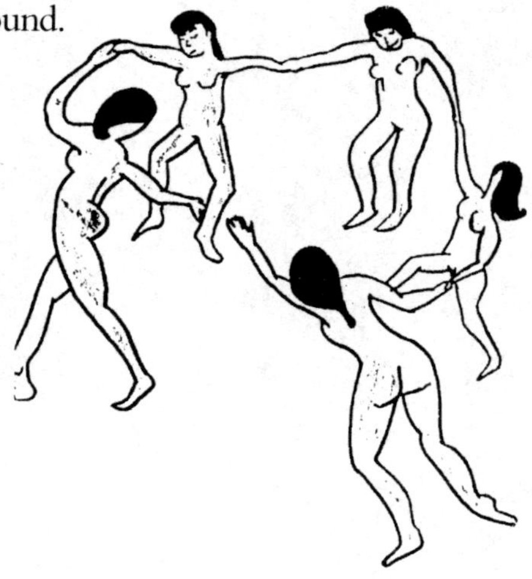

LAUGHTER

When we laugh we show our teeth.
Our cousins the apes do so to show fear.

Hyperventilating we may find we spread this infection,
Others joining in without knowing why,
Sounds exploding from them.

We laugh until we cry sometimes.
Tears and laughter run close,
Just like love and hate.

Yet we enjoy laughing; we need to do so,
We laugh at wit, stupidity, clowns, falls,
The misfortunes of others, banana-skinned.

Laughing can be hysterical, out of control,
Or we may try to suppress it,
Pretend to cough.

Faced with death or life, some laugh defiantly,
Amused, happy, scornful, comical, ridiculous.
Embarrassingly, our bodies and faces contort
On the edge of hysteria.

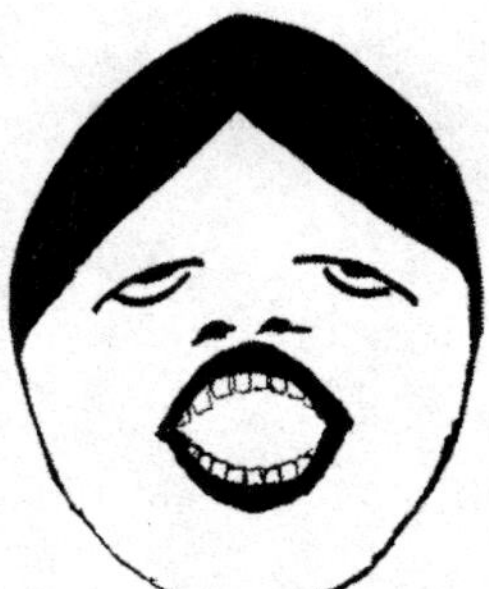

LAYERS

I grow in knowledge of you.
I learn, cautiously, love crossed,

To marvel behind the smile,
At who lives in your body.

Each of us is a mystery, masked,
Friendly, carefree, confident,

To unfold, beyond the image,
Who loves and gives warmth.

Care has armoured my heart,
I move carefully towards Trust,

To disarm myself of experience,
Which hurts my sense of worth.

Each of us, feet on the ground,
Meeting carefully, hopefully

Towards a growing love that's real
Where truth can reign again.

Excitement tempers my tears,
Quietly I talk of betrayals past,

To show you my life, and that
Optimistic, I see Truth in you.

LEARNING BY HEART

I learnt my times-tables,
The Catechism, the prayers,
The dates of the kings and queens,
And some poetry and formulae.

I learnt by heart
That love was good.
The dates were important to us,
I wrote poems and love letters.

I learnt my times over,
That you went away
To another's arms.
I dreamt poems of our past.

I learnt by heart
That love will go
And hearts and dreams can break,
That to love is dangerous.

I learnt to forgive,
That friendships are safer,
And only the poet can truly love,
Dare hold on to loves dream.

I learnt by heart
That we risk too much when
We love without conditions.
The formula is so cruel.

I learnt my heart
Might mend one day,
That another dream of love is
Worth learning by heart.

LEARNING

I learnt your face,
Studied your moods.

I learnt your body,
Rejoiced in the nearness.

I learnt your sex,
Knew your weaknesses.

I learnt your faults
And loved your fineness.

I learnt to love you,
More than myself.

I learnt to know you,
Too well perhaps.

Why then must I un-learn
All that I knew,

Now that you have
Learnt another love?

For to love is to know,
And we cannot un-know.

LEFT

Left, right,

Right angle.
Right on

Right is might.
All right.

Righteous;

The Rite of Mass
Righter than white.

Right of passage,
The Last Rite.

I'm left
Left behind,

Left alone,

Half right,
But really

Left.

LOVE APPLES

My love was cut down before it was ripe,
The apple I gave was all I could give.
It had blossomed and formed, shone in
The sun.

My words like windfalls now rot on the ground.
My love lies in the rack, preserved with others,
To be consumed when the time suits her,
Heady with the cider of fermented love
Apples.

Eat then, or go. Digest what you need.
But the seed of a new love you cannot kill.
It waits for good ground, will grow tall and strong,
New blooms, good fruit, for others
To take:

Eve never gave Adam such an apple.
Its taste brings paradise on earth,
The more you eat of it, the more there is,
But thrown away it ceases to exist
In time.

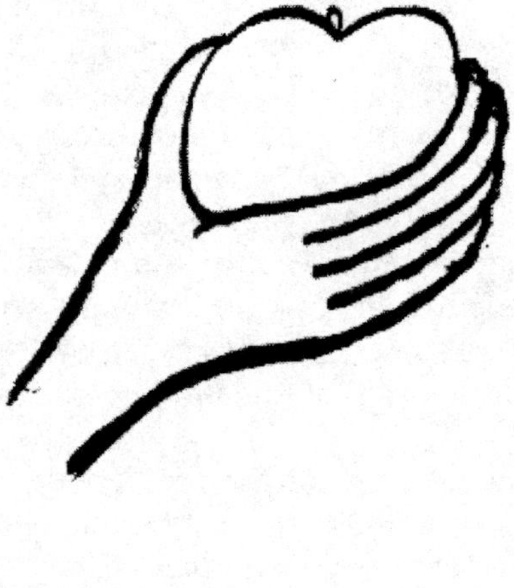

LOVE TORQUE

A metal torque, intricately weaved in
Silver and golden metals, the moon and sun,
Weaved in an open loop, a joining open to fit her,
However big or small she may be.
Open to symbolise freedom, looped,
Curved to symbolise female, a torque.

I bought and wore it for two whole hours,
Round my own left wrist, giving it my warmth.
It said what I wanted to say. I hoped she might
Think of me sometimes as she glanced at it
Just as I had as I wore it. I could give her all,
But can only give her what she can accept.

What colours there seem in spring grasses and the sky.
All that once was so dull, is altered in my mind,
Even the tangled jumble of May time's wild leaves and
Blooms filled my once barren soul with such delight,
Perfumes were more intense, wild blooms now so bright.

A late creativity, a spring in my step, my heart bursting
In this time of hope, of growth, of warm bodies, wet kisses,
With a strong holding passion, an exquisite grace and gentleness.
She wore my gift in her smile, and about her slender wrist.
It shone warm against her soft flesh.

My lover glanced at it, looked up smiling and saw me.
We sat silently staring, each searching the other's eyes.
Her mouth smiled and seemed to want the kiss I ached to offer.
How young we seem as love shines through, past our days.
In my head and heart, my body and soul our circle was complete.

I longed to lay wrapped, like the torque, safe and open with her.
My pillow smells of her hair; lips still tingle when she's gone.
I have learnt and touched her face; she occupies dreams and delights
My mind. I have become forgetful, preoccupied but so alive.

The circle, the talk, the torque, weaves its magic trance,
A crescent moon brings dawn to this transcending love.
Alpha and omega, the spiral dance,
The smiling lips and fingertips.

MAID IN ENGLAND

I was up before the household.
The boy brought in the coals,

And I lit the stove, to boil water
So they might wash:

Hot jugs of water to place in their rooms.
I washed in cold water.

The master in his room was first,
The mistress, last up.

Governess looked after their small children.
The housekeeper and the butler ruled us.

I don't know if the family knew my
Surname, I was Emily to them.

I only had Sunday afternoon free.
I carried; I cleaned, waited and served.

The young Master had his way with me,
As his father had with my mother.

Like her I could say nothing.
I was too frightened of disgrace.

They kept up appearances
I knew my place

They had grand bedrooms,
I had a little attic space.

I had a position in service,
It was on my knees.

So respectable are these hypocrites.
I was made in England …

MASS MEDIA

At Mass I kneel, bend, bow, stand or sit and say the responses,
Believing, I take the Blessed Bread and the Wine, Amen.
I hear the sermon, say the words, even in Latin know
The meaning. It is all so familiar after Catholic Convent.
Silently my Lord whispers to me sometimes,
Inwardly I weep for what we do to one another.
But I hear the voice of God in the wind, without words,
Feel and see the Goddess in the waves and the night sky.
I taste Her lips, touch His Divinity, it's more than as a Trinity.
The God of womankind and Goddess of Mankind is one.
God is the Mother and the Father, Sun and Moon and Earth
Wholly one and Holy One living Divine Spirit.

I cannot feel as Gnostics might, that God is both good and evil,
Extreme, black and white, as perhaps are we; but must agree
She might be both and either: neither male nor female, beyond gender.
As the Almighty Being, the frailties of sex, colour, race and what
Divides people is not part of God, nor is Evil, unless Love be evil.
We see good and evil in all those and in ourselves.
We must, in honesty, know how each exists in us.
So much is grey, not black or white, good or evil, right or wrong.
We can perceive what is kind or cruel, just or unjust,
Great or small, love or hate, live or dead, heaven or hell.
God is hidden in all those we see somewhere too far.
The pain of hell is known to most of us long before we die.

Mediocre "media masses" fill us with so much mulched gloom.
Newspapers always print the bad news, for it sells best. Papers,
TV, radio, magazines tell of mass murder, mass hysteria, mass pickets,
Mass unemployment, and of yet more mass graves, mass destruction.
All is mass indoctrination. Minds are swayed by political lies.
Hearts may be moved as by Band-Aid, an earthquake, a tsunami,
Brief reminders we are all human, brings awareness to the masses.
The Mass Media are there to sell, not necessarily to offer the truth.
Truth is hard to find when belief is challenged by facts.
Even the existence of God is put to the question by science,
But is Science the new hubris, this new god, the truth?
We, the masses, will not find any answer from the Media.

MIDDLE AGES

Fathers and mothers are beginning to die
Middle Age has
Crept upon us.

Even Police Inspectors begin
To look young

Idealists are become reactionaries.
Beauties grown plump, invisible,
Or wrinkled.

Late beauty in some once unlined faces,
Stories mapped in smile
Or frown lines.

We grow weary of work, feel a need for family.
Grandchildren surprise us
With Grand-names.

Wisdom is the province of the aged,
But we are not old enough to be wise,
Or wise enough to be old.

We cling to the innocence of the young,
Pretend the book still has many pages
Before it will close.

Middle age spreads like bindweed.
We are amazed by its inevitability.

Insecure, of a certain age, life-paused
In-between, neither young, nor old,

On the sharp
Edge of the fence.

MIRROR

Mirrored before me,
Two faces
Yours and mine.

You are gone now.
I still
See your image.

Reflections
Follow me
Everywhere.

Neither shadows
Nor pictures,

But mirrors of you;
Broken now,

In thousand-fold
Shards of sharp glass;

Cold to touch,
Cutting my

Caressing fingers
Held out to them.

MIRROR CARP

Seeing a small dark fish among the goldfish,
I ask the pet shop man, "What is it?"
"A mirror carp" was the reply. I could see why.
She had large silver scales, far fewer that other carp,
Placed apparently randomly around her back and sides.

Like all carp, dark pigment above, light below.
Yet in the grey-brown darkness of the ventral surface
Was deep green, black, onyx and sage.
Along the silver dorsal area were white and gold and yellow.
A fleshy barb each side of her low mouth helped her taste for food.

The scales of a fish show growth rings, like those of a tree,
Hers were wide apart, showing rapid growth.
She didn't appear to know fish remained a size
Suitable for their environment. She just kept growing.
She outgrew all her companions in my fish-tank.

She trained me, like Pavlov's dogs, to feed her
Each time she went to the right-hand corner of the tank.
She ate more, and quicker, than all the other fish.
Grown eventually too long for the aquarium,
She only had one of the original fish to share it with.

What do you do with a fish that simply grows and grows?
Unkind souls suggested "Try grilling - with parsley sauce",
Others, "release into a pond", or "get a bigger tank",
"Convert the bathroom to a fish farm", "move to a larger place".
She had simply grown too big for her fins.

MISS TAKES

Know your needs from your wants.
Wisdom is the survival of the soul.

Learn to feed the body and the mind.
To live with credit, not on credit.

An account is kept by our conscience,
To bounce back, to check yourself.

Invest your time and thought wisely;
For we have a joint Account with God.

There is no place for loss or misery
One must be the flame, not the moth.

A wise person learns by her mistakes,
A wiser woman learns by the mistakes

Of others.

MOMENTS AND MOVEMENTS

First seen a stranger, an academic, and an intellectual,
A Tutor? Thought she might teach me. Sat nearby,
Then a smile, a greeting, shook hands. Liked her looks,
Her style, what a musical voice, culture, laughter,
Careful intelligent words. We touched that first time.
She wanted a lift to the station. I learnt she was married.

A kiss goodbye, waved, and then watched her walk away.
Saw grace in her movement, liked her words and thoughts,
Her dress sense, her good sense, recognised her vulnerability,
We quietly spoke of divorces, children, worries we shared.
Some friendly new students passed and smiled greetings.
Later, a party, She brought music with her; always does.

She led the dance. I held her hand. The dance began.
We six circle-dancing women formed a circle on the floor,
A candle centred between us, energy from hand to hand.
I watched her dancing feet; her left hand in my right
I tried to follow her steps distracted by her smile.
It seemed I turned her on too, couldn't believe it, such madness,

Was it destiny, reality? The moon was full.
Was it lunatic to love again?
When she had listened to my poems she said she'd
Thought me freer than she, yet she seemed to move without weight.
We danced, body against body, clothes between us,
Swayed by the music and our rhythms.

First lovemaking, before those words, "I love you".
The forbidden words. The words we could not subdue.
Wet, so wet, held tight, exploring kisses, eyes and hands
Set aside the clothes. I felt shy, but her smile reassured.
Each in turn would come and come again.
We learn each other. We tell our stories.

Moments and movements we share.

MOON GODDESS

The Moon Goddess, from her dark side,
Sees her children, her daughters
In the Sun.

With men it's being; Women it's giving;
Offering homage in
The darkness;

Women are the luminaries of
Moonbeams.

It is we who carry her gentle
Healing, loving power
To her children.

The man in the moon's imaginary face
Sees the Goddess, Ruler
Of the Moon.

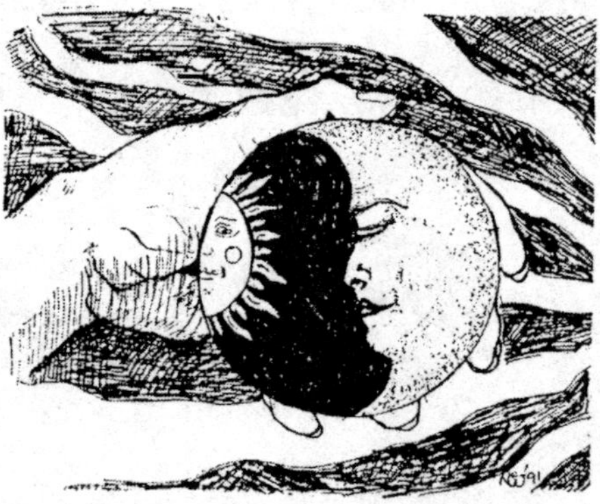

Moon gravity pulls fluid tides of seas
And lakes, and our bodies
And our minds.

Her force draws irresistibly,
Attracts the waters and fluids
Of our life.

The sun is gaseous, not solid.
A great light and heat radiation is
Sent out to us.

It is the progenitor, but burns
Earth's life - so hot it kills if
Drawn too close.

Yet the sun is but a small typical star
In the Milky Way, in this our small,
But great Galaxy.

MOON LINKS

A telephone call. She'd gone home,
Away across the cold
Gray North Sea.

I thought of her and was wondering
If she was also
Thinking of me.

Yes, I'd phone her.
Damn the expense,
Had to hear the
Music of her voice.

Looking at the clear-lit night sky,
I saw the full moon: an idea
Came to me,

I dialled her number,
"Yes", she answered,
We spoke to each other.
It was so good.

"Look at the moon,
Through your window"
I said, "It's full
In the South East.

So that both were at once
Looking at this bright light,
As our Words joined us.

In sound and sight,
We two lovers were
Doubly connected thanks to
The Moon Link.

RIPPLES

A lover's tears fall into the pool,
Circle ripples destroys their reflections.

This mirror is lost in a moment,
To return with time.

A stone dropped into night water
Ripples its surface,

Makes the moon's light bend,
Moonlets bobbing in its blackness;

A moment that's lost.

Stand still a while near water, lovers,
So you may see

The golden ripples in sunlight and
Through its surface

To the deep below,
And what might be.

A tear-filled eye cannot clearly see,
But allows others to see within.

Cover your pain with still waters
So others may see you smile.

MORSE MESSAGE

Dot dot dot dash dash dash dot dot dot

... _ _ _ ...

A film together, "Desert Hearts", me still in my desert,
The passion of the lovers, knowing their joy and the pain, in
What we could still be.

We talk of our separate days, of different journeys joined
In talk of work and feelings,
A catch-up Time.

The telecom connection broken, an accident of placement cut us off,
Lost in work, time-forgotten. Time gone, no warning
No watch worn or kept,

Another afternoon spent alone, Daylight almost gone. Spring's passing,
Easter's almost here, I'm musing, thinking hopefully,
Anticipating, Passion Sunday.

Shared a gourmet meal at a table for three, then, well fed, back to my solitude,
But some appetite still un-sated. A double bed for one, king-sized,

No dreaming, no urgent hand, no soft skin, no gentle touch.
Crystal cold beauty surrounds me in days and fossilised nights

Marking time, in one place, as life changes. Not trusting my Trust,
Aware of hopeless unpaid labour, unused skills.

Weeds begin to grow in my path and seeds remain in their packets.
Dead fish, photos of skeletal forms. I'm on the point of resignation,

I see joy, but saddened by easy solitude, I wonder why we live and die alone?
But, Oh, what memories, sun-setting on my needs, my laughter and hopes.

A comet draws near our World this evening, in the early night sky
I touch the stars, and fly still holding her so close.

MOTHER EARTH

We are told an ozone hole had appeared over Antarctica,
Summers became dryer and warmer, winters wetter and
Windy.

A Greenhouse effect, neatly calculated by our scientists,
Too late to reverse or correct. Carbon Dioxide levels
Rise.

The ice is melting, the sea is rising. No snow on the piste.
Holiday plans change for the rich, now low islands are to
Drown.

Forests and lakes lie wasted by the acid rain, flue gasses,
Car exhausts, aerosol sprays, insecticides, and fertilisers,
People.

Sewage, concentrating nitrogenous wastes, greens the oceans.
Slime, sludge floats on the surface, rubbish litters deepest sea
Beds.

Infant mortality reduced - our species spreads over the land.
Rain forests felled, the rain takes away the little soil. People
Drown

Soil clogs the rivers, whilst the land is stripped. Some species
Extinct as environments go, to fill museums and zoos. A last
Ditch.

Technology has unbalanced nature for all species, not just
Plants, or other animals. We too are in jeopardy. Oh Mother
Earth.

MY FAULT I THINK? ...

★ *To be read without irony.*

I am sorry,
It was my fault.

My fault that you
Could not force me to change.
I did not love you enough.

My fault I could not share you.
I failed to give you space.

My fault I missed you.
I cannot suppress real love.

My fault I have been hurt,
It happens all the time.

My fault you hate me.
You need to forget.

My fault letting go is hard,
You are too important.

My fault I would not forbid you.
We each deserve our decisions.

My fault I awake in tears.
Yes, it's all my fault.

It was my fault until now,
And will be.

I cannot be someone else.

That's my fault.

NEEDLES

A trail of green needles, embedded in jumper, carpet, cushions, the chair backs.
The vacuum cleaner will surely smell of pine forests for some time, will need
Emptying of coniferous Christmas debris, dusty glitter, and tinsel morsels.
The mistletoe berries, semen-like, are squashed, stuck, with dog hair and crumbs,
Under the centre light and the doorway.
Dust lined marks where cards stood, cards bundled to sort next year's Card List,
Some quite beautiful, others awful. Skeletal tree sacrificed to Christmas, once
Central, now dumped, undecorated in the back yard. Watch it die, planted
In the chalky soiled back garden, roots killed earlier by the grower.
There's a silver glass ball under the piano.

Boxes of torn brightly coloured wrapping paper which may come in handy next year,
Ready for the attic, with tree lights which will tangle and stop working of their
Own accord. Decorations re-boxed, hurriedly, reveal undecorated spaces, a
Decorating job to do later. There are Christmas wrappers in my attic
Going back to the old days of string.
Yes Christmas comes but once a year, but for several weeks, that's excessive.
It is a time of excess, followed by the bills, the melancholia; trying to lose weight;
Resolutions. So many last minute rushes, such complex planning, resembling
A seduction, a daydreamed love affair, in which all ends Happily Ever After,
Promising the Joys of Christmas to Come.

Holly, berries still bright, leaves darker, dry - dusty, to light the fire with,
To finally feel that simple, splendid satisfaction as Christmas is packed up and
Put away or burnt, yellow flaming and crackling, destroyed with the false hope
And sentimentality that allows you to believe that none of those you love will
Disappoint you this year. Some always do.
Remembrances of Christmas past. Absent friends. Come all ye. Father Christmas
Doesn't come here any more, now children are grown up. He didn't come down
My chimney at least. I had it swept in case he might. Perhaps the sight of my tights
At the end of my bed put him off, or the hearth filled log fire left burning in the empty
Shimmering beauty of Christmas Eve.

Cards from friends you deleted, making you feel guilty; and no cards from those who
Deleted you, to make you wonder why? Increased weight and waistline, decreased
Fiscal credibility! Turkey cooked twenty-seven different ways, making you long for
Bread and cheese. Needles in my heart. Each time my susceptibilities opened wide,
Childlike by Christ's reality, I weep. The carols, candles, colours, care:
Surely Christmas should be each day, but could we keep the pace?
Seasons Greetings. Needles in my heart.
Feeling thirteenth Nighted.

MY LOVER'S NOISY BOWELS

There's thunder in the air.

We are so close, I sometimes don't know if it's she or me
Who makes these loud abdo' noises?
A great rush and a drain like gurgle.

We can't blame the dog always, he sleeps downstairs anyway,
He dreams sometimes, scratches, but breaks wind with lethal silence.

No it is the equivalent of the dawn chorus, almost a religious experience
In its sombre acoustic prelude to and accompany of sleep.

Sometimes it is like a thunderstorm. I'm sure it's not me.
People don't do things like that in Hove.

She's never been the same since reading Chaucer.
It's liberated her mind and her bowels,

Like a Born-again-vegetarian she thunders through the night.
It is odd though that I can still hear it when I am alone.

Perhaps it's the late night cup of tea.
Whatever, I'm sure it's not me.

Chaucer was obviously from Brighton.

★ *Alice actually lives in Hove.*

CHAUCER

NO CHANGE

"How are things for you?" the ex-lover asked nervously.
Dumped by her, alone I'd wept.

"How are things for you?" I asked later. I'm told, "We're fine".
Together THEY walked the beach.

How are things for you? I think to myself - No change –
I reply, knowing everything is different.

"How are things for you?" was the question.
"Fine", I reply, knowing I lie to both of us.

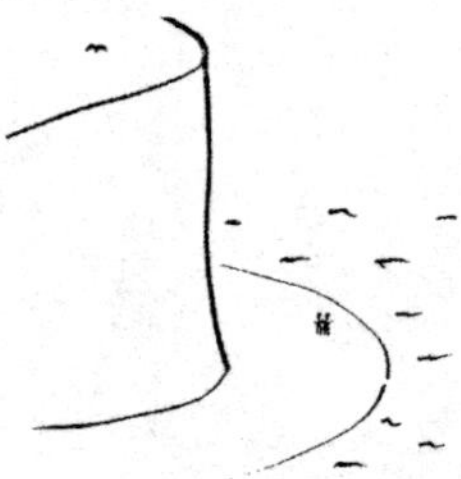

NOW HOW

Don't say you'll love me
    Only love me now.

Don't say you do love me,

Only tell me how.

Don't say you will leave me
    Only leave me now.

Don't go now and leave me,
    Only show me how.

Don't try to remember me,
    Only don't forget.

Don't say it was forever,
    Only don't say yet.

NOTIONS

Went on holiday
With her this time.
Visited old haunts,
Walked by the canals.
Lovers going through
The motions.

Hoped it gave
Her pleasure then.
Wondered when
It would end this
Time, unlikely false
Emotions

Tried to please,
With her this time.
Danced together:
Showed all I knew
To her: her excessive
Devotions.

Neither really
Loved, each needed.
She took more,
Sucked me dry,
It's time to end these
Notions.

WHEN

When I, hold you in my arms, I believe,
When I, feel your hand in mine, I believe,
When I, look deep into your eyes, I believe.
I believe when we kiss, touch, make love,
I believe when we look at bluebells
I believe when we wake up together.

Oh, When our eyes speak, our mouths see,
When our ears feel and our fingers hear, when
You stay although you are going, I believe.
We are free spirits, closer than before,
In love, in honesty, pain and confusions
Your problems are mine, are truly shared.

Now we must face them alone, like a death,
Now we want life together, we are parting
Now we each understand but can't solve it.
If mermaids fly and centaurs swim,
If men cry and women are strong
If snow's in May and green England browns,

Then one will find a way, not be away,
But be together, not to a parting, sadly,
Not too apart, but two a part, as one.
What paradox, what dilemma, what madness!
That brief spring day love, flower scented,
To hold in memory against this winter cold.

I love you, am in love in sweet moments,
Yet salt tears burn my cheeks as you go,
I push away, not you, but this reject pain.

NOVEMBER

It is time to close the garden,
The frosts of November have come.

Last mowing done, leaves cleared away,
Flowerpots inside, seeds all gathered.

The snails and the slugs and the toads,
Large for winter, huddle under things.

Ready. Late blooms surprise us,
The pink rose still scents sweet, of summer.

All pruned; weeds cleared; soil layed bare.
Bonfired, twigs burnt - smoky - ash spread,

All tidied, polite, ready for the snows,
The ground dug clear, cut flowers bought now.

Plants need no weather forecast,
Leaves fall when they are ready.

The blossoms, nature's summer dresses
Are folded away, for next time.

OLD FLAMES

The high jagged flames play almost to heaven itself,
A midnight bonfire; the golden sparks fly skywards;

A smoky halo of pink and yellow in the deep night sky.
Extra stars drift upwards, a flux of moving sparklet lights.

A crackle of fracturing twigs and branches glows red,
In the heart of the fire roars a glorious golden flame.

Black shadow shapes slide silhouetted against firelight,
As they dance, warming, their golden faces turned to it.

Around the clearing, still growing branches steam in the
Radiated heat, highlighted by the red roaring bonfire:

Twigs rustle leafless in the up draught caused by the roar
Of the fire, and crackle their destruction and oxidation.

These living twigs and branches stand out stark against a
Starlit sky, Chinese black against paler celestial lights.

They pass painted by advancing night through purples and
Mauves to indigo. Our fine fire dwarfs the dear bright lunar-light.

Its smoky cloud obscures the silver-sliver moon-disc.
Lunar light seems gone to its fire-worked end.

Menaced by the fire this moon might, like the branches,
Ignite and burst showering the sky with tiny moonlets,

Old flames like the great fire and the constant Moon,
Like sunlight reflected in water, are gold and silver.

With the passing years I still enjoy the memory of those
Old flames.

**The author loves a bonfire and several "old flames"*

ON THE BEACH

On the beach I found her,
A great grey body stranded.
Seagulls had pecked at her skin.
Her eye moved when I drew near.

She was alive when I found her.
A sea goddess had landed.
Barnacles had encrusted her skin,
Her body scarred by a great fight.

I took water in my hands to bathe
Her poor face, sanded, bleached.
She had striven to free herself,
As the tide had left her there.

Her eye watched me as I tried so hard
To keep her body cool, as it dried out
By unfamiliar sunshine, skin cracked.
This air breather overheats, dies on land.

Her dark eye and my eyes meet.
Hers from deep acceptance glazed.
Helpless I watched her as she died.
I could not turn that so slow tide.

Alone I could not lift her, leviathan,
Back to the oceans where she dwelt.
She'd roamed three quarters of the globe,
The surfaces and deeps of the oceans.

Now she was to lie dead and stinking in the sun.

ONE OF THOSE DAYS

Ever had one of those days?
Got, up, vacuumed and dusted the whole house,
Sat down for a black coffee and fag,

Then when putting on my rings, realised after a prolonged search,
It narrowed down to the fact I'd vacuumed up an irreplaceable garnet ring,
Of considerable sentimental value.

So sifted through the dust, filth and a tangle of dog hairs.
He'd been dead a week, but I could still smell his doggy smell.
"All that's left now", was my thought,

"Dust to dust, ashes to ashes"
And the cat's gone missing a week.
I began to take it personally.

Sadness, then off to do my counselling.
The car door handle came off in my hand.
Then, although new, the leaking radiator was empty again.

Got tap water and topped it up. Started the Renault, changed into first,
I found myself holding the gear-leaver knob in my left hand.
Struggled with it all morning.

Felt considerably better after giving my counselling session.
Hope my client also did. I usually felt exhausted,
Even very depressed, after an hour with her.

Got out of car, looked at my hand, the rings all back in place,
Including the one rescued from the cleaner-bag, and
Tripped over the kerbstone.

ONE WHO GOES BEFORE ... *AGAIN**

"If I should die before you, remember me.
If the soft breeze should caress your cheek
On a spring morning, or late of an evening
It is perhaps my breath,"

For I will be with you always
Thoughts of you fill me with dread,
Lest I should lose you.

No, death shall not brag to us.
It is to be outlived, out-loved.

Out of our depth in life we swim through
Our days; and drift together in slumber sleep;
That brief death. It breaks and I find
You are warm beside me.

Anger rarely kills our hope of love.
Laughter long sounds through our separations.

Memories, reminiscences, grow as we gather
Shared time for old age.

The one we chose to love becomes an anchor:
I an anchorite; hold you on no pedestal;

I see quite clearly our differences,
Yet I rejoice at our time

Shared, not wasted,
Wonderful lost minutes.

For time flies above cheerful clouds,
Taking us to our end; shared ...

**The first stanza was from a letter to a sweetheart in the American Civil War*
It is about being joined although parted, even by death.

OUR PATH*

A walk down wild garlic scented paths
Through bright young trees and weeds.
Fresh scythed wild flowers and grasses in
Our path.
A look through a square window cut in the
Green brown gneiss wall to a gentle sea.
Hot Alderney sun, slows our booted stride,
Hands held.

A beach of rocks four billennia old, strewn
Untidy boulders, seaweed bladders, jetsam,
Seagull feathers beached. Boots off, foam
Round toes.
A cigarette in the sun, sea stacks before us.
Guillemots and puffins fly cautiously above.
Epidote green, hornblende pinks, porphyries
To collect.

She sat on, whilst I explored, hammer in hand,
Touching old Earth's crust with reverent fingers.
Boots wet now, I left the rest to be with her on
The beach.
Clambered through sea-arch, cliffs high above.
She sat in sunlight, boots off, eating slowly,
Staring out towards England, with thoughts of
Our home.

We sat together, sisters on the rocks, upright,
Touched finger tips. Others came and ate nearby.
We knew we had soon to climb up the cliff with
Our rocks.
I hurt in my body, but my heart flew with the gulls.
I was happy as we walked together up the steep path,
And ached for the time we might make love, flying,
Fingers linked.

**This is about a Geological Society Field trip to Guernsey with a sweetheart.*

OUT FOR A BOUNDARY

When is a boundary a barrier?
We each have our limits, clear or unclear.
These can be set aside when in love.

Time, with brooding familiarity,
Makes them impediments, walls,
And intolerable fortresses.

They become issues, criticisms,
Nagging at the sufferer and at the
Other's less strict walls.

A clinging love can be a form of oppression,
But the freedom one needs, if not met
By consideration can box-in a person.

But a request for commitment is reasonable,
If too much freedom is required by the other.

Idealistically love has no boundary,
In the real world boundaries must allow

A meeting of the needs of both and each,
equally. If not considered, love morphs to
confrontation.

Is this need of a boundary a just impediment
To love? A surfeit of independence is surely
separation?

Is compromise always a loss
If both regain a common cause?

THE CONTRACT

Boundaries are needed,
I can't feel the ground.
I fear I have lost you,
Everything has changed.

I'll do what I can,
But you must do as
I ask to reassure me.
I need to know you care.

There are the children,
Retirement and my book,
Our home and memories,
Our life still has meaning.

I have thought about it,
Little else.
I'm obsessed.
Oh don't go!

What do you want,
I must know?

Why can't I do that for you?
I have written the Contract,
It's as much as I'll concede.

Do your part and I'll do mine.
I need security,
Not to lose you.

- *This is what happens when two counsellors get together!*

OUT FOR A DUCK

Grey afternoon drizzle on wind whipped waters,
Ochre wet, impenetrable to light, licking the shore.

Mallards move towards our bread,
Norfolk Broads this autumn afternoon.

Boats tied along shoreline empty of tourists.
Windmill still, in the distance, double sails.

We see wide-eyed, wide sky, wet wind-washed
Walls of broken flints, ice aged and timeless.

Season's changes slip by, swans neck towards us.
They so cautiously feed from our nervous hands.

I am conscious of the dead duck, in the boot
Of the car, which a fellow motorist hit.

This drake with iridescent green neck, fine feathered
Thoughts only of his mate, out for a duck,

Now for our pot, our sauce to enrich him.
I feel ashamed of our carnivorous practicality.

Somewhat sad eyed; we consider orange sauce a good idea.
Beneath those gorgeous feathers a duck is quite small,

He bowled his last maiden over, never ducked in time,
Soundless this wild life ended.

The swans look quite big …

**Road kills are a good source of game, but must not be deliberate!*
Ever tried squirrel?

PAST BEARING

The air is heady
With the scent of roses,

Yet the sky has greyed,
And a dull humid

Blanket of air overcasts
The curving land.

Past bearing.

Ladies try not to glow,
But actually sweat.

I walk like a pregnant
Rhinoceros.

I feel more like an
Old woman every day,

Past bearing.

REFLECTIONS

Reflect on your reflection.
Yes, take a hundred lines,
In your face, around your eyes,
Lining the way of the world.

Mirrored in a face's map
Is its pain and laughter.

The faces of the young are
Not yet pruned by life.

Prune away care and ambition,
Chip away and make your hay.

Let eyes sparkle out ideals,
Show your not-yet-lost dreams

PETALS

When she stood close to me
I noticed that her nipples
Like mine, had become
Hard erect, obvious.

We were arranging a vase of flowers together.
Their scents and our perfumes had mingled.
I felt quite dizzy

Her large eyes sought mine as
She felt me stare at her.
She knew that I knew she
Was also turned on.

"Are you cold?" I asked, my hand
Placed carefully on top of hers.
She turned her hand to
Gently hold my arm.

I brushed imaginary petals
From her dress, and from mine.
We stood close. I could feel her
Breath's warmth on my neck.

I placed her hand on my thigh,
Wished we were naked, her other
Hand on my shoulder.
We kissed slowly and deeply.

A pink petal drifted to the ground.

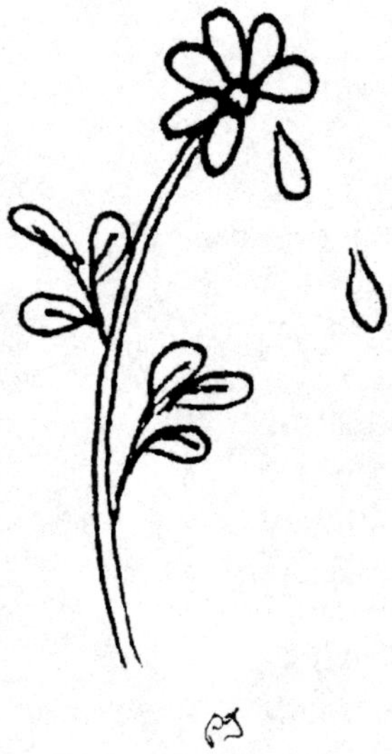

PUT OUT THAT LIGHT

★*Who'd be an insomniac? Word games sometimes help.*

Are you depressed?
It's depressing, deep resting.
Death is deep resting.

Poetry is often a flight from insomnia.
I dears, get ideas.
Use of the pun,

Flights of the pen,
Ancient and Modern,
Penultimate thoughts,

That time before sleep.
In the attic of my head is lumber,
Fearful of time lost in slumber,

I try to build with words.
Awake, a wake for
Memories of the past.

Past tense, still tense.
Tension; Pension;
Time's is getting on.

This sleepless night must end!
Working when you're tired
Is a quick way to get fired.

Dawn chorus fills me with dread,
The night becomes day.
Purple light ending night.

With the Sun I will rise,
Cannot fight daylight.
No chance to put out that light.

R.S.P.C.A. DOG

* *The author has always had a dog, usually called Oliver.*

First seen shivering, fearful in a filthy cage,
The pup, starved, skinny, eyes stuck with dry tears,
Man-wrecked, tortured, terrified: we both rage.
This brown, cringing, young life, almost maimed by fear.

A hand offered, dog cowers, oceans in deep brown eyes.
Seeing his pain, knowing my own, I feel our ties.
Both were hurt, alone, unnerved, must reclaim trust.
Loving again, patiently, gently, we must, we must.

Door opened, he bolts from the ghosts of his past.
Plays 'Catch me if you can'; he was too fast.
Shy even to feed, until hunger draws him in:
He began to know he had space, and had his tin.

On South Down Way, to Chanctonbury, became a real hound.
He'd sniffed; he'd peed, lurched, and leapt over the ground,
Watching me, now his 'top dog'; aware where I strode:
Circling to and fro, round and round, peripheral to my road.

Tired; lying in a grassy bed; green all around;
Skylarked blue above the soil scented ground,
Feeling a brown shape, a warm panting thing
Pressed against me, I saw eyes shining, heart on wing.

He lay by me that first time, and so many more:
Learnt to trust, come to me when hungry, or hurt, and to adore.
Fed from my hand, and my heart, gave me such welcome.
He'd be waiting my return, tail wagging to see his 'mum'.

Asleep on chair or bed, knowing no danger with me there,
Others come and all is changed, still a while he'd stare,
Gauging if things were safe, if he might be given space.
He'd smell the hand, the legs; seek danger in the face.

Chocolate overcame most fear, a genuine joy.
Paw raised, he'd beg, and receive: "Oh, clever boy!"
He could sit, heel, stay, go down, and smile:
He drank real ale, would sneeze tipsy a while.

RELIVING MAYDAY ON CHANCTONBURY

Before the sun has risen birds start to sing,
Buds begin to open; leaves turn eastwards;
A hint of red outlines the easterly landscape.
White haw blossom pinked by the glow.
Grows yellow by sun ascendant in the sky.

Insolent almost, four town-bred girls' faces,
See, marvel at its rising, just on time, as ever.
Mysterious woods, un-shadowed behind them
Accessed by its light and warmness, promising
Summer, heat radiates away the dawn-dew of May.

Friesians stir, sway, stand and sticky lick the car,
Taking in the night's pure droplets on long pink tongues.
Sleeping still, the Weald, re-coloured by daylight,
Streetlights still on, show town-in-country:
Where man is unaware of Mayday morning.

Morris-men morrissed, moved on after midnight,
Bells jingling jangling, up and down the hillside.
A march of time, timeless; dance to the summer,
Winter done, washed down with real Harvey's Ale.
All left, leaving only four women to sleep under stars.

She put daisies in my hair, like the Judas kiss,
A good act betraying, poisoned, poised in my memory.
May is a time of change; the Queen is crowned,
The fool and the dragon leap and dance around.
Old folks remember times gone by; sing the old song.

Walk winnikin for ever-young lovers,
Walk the ring round; rings on fingers to forget.
Dawn brings a new day, another lover,
Druids, Mithrans, Christians stand and marvel
At Beltane on Chanctonbury, it stays in my soul.

'God save the Queen', 'God save the Ring', dance on.
Trees; now flattened by hurricane; lie like felled troops;
Roots upturned scar the earth, tangles of Roman tiles, flints,
Rubbish, debris of centuries; the Ring profile ruffled.
Saplings see their chance, a space for growth, in new light

REVOLTING

There's few things as revolting as pubic hair that's moulting:

As breasts that are sagging, or legs that need lagging:

As treading barefoot on a slug, or after party puke on your rug;

As toe nail clippings in an ashtray, or house keys that have gone astray.

As cat pee in the bath, or dog poop on your path.

As creatures squashed by cars, or a bending workman showing his arse.

As fag ends in congealed egg, or an old crone showing too much leg.

As teenage romances in Aussie soaps, or TV adverts designed for dopes.

As being told you're sixty-five, or feeling old and only half-alive.

As maggots in your cheese, or dogs infested with fleas.

As a lip-sticked cupid's bow, or a car that just won't go.

As used condoms and sea-borne S.T.s', or the scent of sewage on the breeze.

As a woman who's a lush, or Christmas shopping in a rush.

As hairy warts on a nose, or bunions on your toes.

As hot flushes without warning.

Or a man in the morning.

**Sorry chaps!*

RIGHT OF WAY

Was she going my way? I wondered.
Was she straight bi' or gay? I pondered.
Was she going to stay?

The guests had all gone,
Yet she lingered on.

We cleared up together.

Should I make her a bed on the floor?
Could I offer her mine, or more?

Did she know I wished her to stay?
Just what exactly could I say?

Then her hand was on mine,
Oh! Her lips looked divine!

They opened up, together.

The party was over, our time to decide,
Dancing all done, not so much to hide.

The meeting of eyes spoke words that I sought,
Tonight she's going to stay, or so I thought

Fingertips touching, my fears almost gone
We kissed like great lovers, became as of one

Went up to bed together.

RIVER WALKS

Riverbank walked from Arundel, dog leading.
Swift high banked Arun, muddy grey chalk water,
The wildfowl water meadows green,
We strode together towards our days ahead.

Electric lit canals, bridge beyond bridge, Amstel,
Amsterdam lovers boated and ambled slowly,
Linked by day and night, by Sun and moonlight.
Gabled houses crowd to see us buy flowers.

Bookstalls, antiques, prints, postcards to browse,
Lining Paris River, cafes on boulevard corners for
Coffee, brandy and Gitanes. Watched the world go by.
We sat and talked, and walked on, and sat again.

Lewes Ouse, down the hill to Cliffe, bonfire night;
Followed the Vikings, their torches burnt our way,
The great fire, crowds roared, we clung to each other.
Tar barrel extinguished in dark water, smelled saltpeter.

Same river, Mayday, dancers processing, bells ringing,
Sun-shining for the May Queen, we followed as always.
Something in your face told me what I already knew.
We spoke and parted; you walked from my life.

Rivers of tears have fallen from my eyes since.
No embankment contains that salt stream.
Water still flows to the sea, watched by lovers.
I stand with others by other rivers, alone.

Reflected there in the water is your face by mine,
Invisible to others, it fades and is carried off by that stream.
Arm in arm I walk with a stranger, sadly.
Oh, where have you gone, my riverbank walker?

Canal or riverbanks were our pavements.

RODMELL GIRLS

Virginia Woolf, the she-wolf-bitch,
Was she Madonna, virgin, hag or witch?

A gender warrior, she made some fearful.
Yet vulnerable in her raging fear of

Her own sadness, she sought an end of that pain
When she walked into the River Ouse,

Her large pockets filled with flint stones
She'd chosen, or found or been given.

We each have such stones, which we carry.
They're our own madness, our sadness,

As we wearily walk towards those cold grey
Drowning rivers, to try for an escape.

These stones are marked "Love me", "Should do",
"Ought to", "Emptiness", "Different", "Despair".

They stop us from running, flying or swimming.
So toothless we sink, drowning in black despair.

Throw them away! Watch them bounce on the waves.
Sink them! Wave goodbye to these heavy weights

And choose life!

* *Woolf lived at Rodmell, in the valley of the river Ouse, Sussex. Died 28/3/1941. Her body was found down stream at Piddinghoe, stones in her pockets.*

ROUND PILLOW

That time was a flight from memory and grief.
I saw her needs; knew it was not love again.
Unsure I ever saw her; not forgetting that time
Shared with another.
Once we made a bed, lay united till judgement
Break, excellent and fair, on round pillow, round
Arms, round bodies; round and infinite the ground ...
She went away soon.
Easily let go the rage, the sorrow for false love.
Looked for daylight reflected in mourning sky:
Laughed cynically, wept gently for that hope
I even still felt.

SAFE

My safe has been broken open,
A safebreaker has left hope.
In the breakers yard.
Breakers crash over my granite
Groynes in the gathering storm
Salt spray on my cheeks.

Secure as a boat on a thread
In a hurricane, that fragile
Line still holds fast.
The mountain melts,
The Vulcan fire erupts,
The hard words,

Love was no safe haven,
No secure hope.
Its heat hurts the calm.
My granite melts
In that heat, there is no relief
Those sharp shard crystals cut belief.

SCHOOL DINNERS

Salad, one might believe, was safe.

I recall a particular school lunch, where,
On one plate I had an annelid, gastropod,
An insect, an arachnid and a coleopterid!
The worm, snail, ant, spider, and beetle
Which lay in my lettuce showed how truly
Organic school dinners could be.

I was grateful that, unlike my friend,
My worm was at least entire.
To find half a worm is after all twice
As bad, rather than half as horrid.

The lady who served lunches was known
As 'Dead -Eyed Doris'. We speculated
As to whether her glass eye replaced
One lost in the amazing organic lunches
She prepared.

The relish with which she served
Spotted Dick and Toad in the Hole,
Made us wonder as to the fate of her
Absent husband.

Perhaps though, he, poor man, had
Found his way to the compost heap,
Rather than our 'whole food'
School dinners.

WWF

SCRUBBERS ON THE RAILWAYS

★ *With the demise of British Rail have things improved? A Swedish Scrubber is not a Scandinavian lady of lose morals, but is a machine for removing leaves from rails etc.*

A Swedish Scrubber in a war against leaves,
For a leaf can stop a modern railway train.

Line-side vegetation is a green finger of our
Conserved countryside each side of the line,

A wilderness, which bewilders our railwaymen
With the surprise of autumn leaves and winds.

Electric or diesel engines have only a fraction
Of the traction of the old steam engine's weight,
Action and reaction.

A one hundred and seventy ton steam train loco
Had plenty of traction; snowdrifts or leaves
Were pushed aside.

Now, the shock, we have shiny, swift Electrified Stock,
Unheated modernity is stopped in its tracks by an
Unfamiliar leaf.

They are sorry and do apologise …

Nobody thought of the unforeseen circumstance of
Autumn leaves

Or the wrong sort of snow.

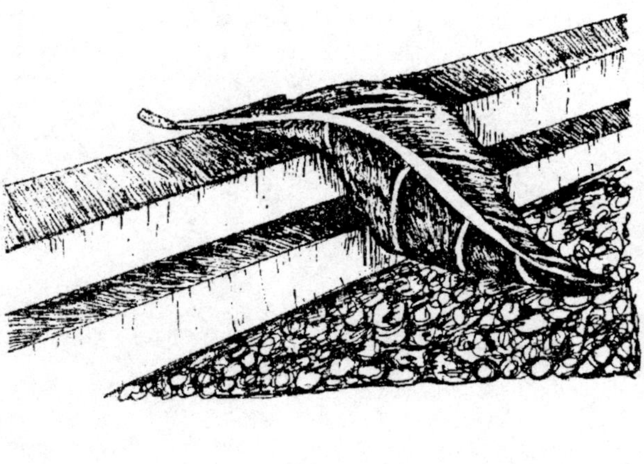

SEEING IS NOT BELIEVING

Our eyes are our windows to the world,
And the world's windows to our souls.
Look hard into an eye and you will

See yourself,
Imaged.
Not the soul
Of one you seek to see.

We rarely see each other clearly.
Optical aids do not help,
Even to see oneself.

Seek to see oneself in a mirror,
And one sees a flat reflection.
Reflect on what you see with

Closed
Eyes

SENSE

I had lost my voice,

Lost sight of the truth,

Could not smell the roses,

Lost track of what was said,

Lost my taste for life,

And lost touch with reality.

I've found a voice,

I can see the truth,

Smell flower's fragrances,

But I hear the silence,

It tastes of bitter gall.

I'm touched by memories.

I sing this song of love

And accept what I see.

Smells evoke remembrances,

So I listen for whispers

Lips parted; smile tastefully;

My hand held by a friend.

SEPTEMBER

The hopes of May's blooms are turned to seeds.
Fallen apples rot on the ground, sweet and ripe.
Invertebrates feed, multiply and fill the air and ground.
Spring is the time for mammals, save man, the all-rounder.
Fecund nature revels in its success before winter's ravages.
Multitudes of greens grow and glow over all the countryside.

A day comes, with chill and a hint of frost in the morning air.
Leaves begin to fall, before the trees are browned off with summer,
Yet, as they fall, new buds already await next spring.
How fortunate we are our Mother Nature gave us seasons,
To section our year, and bring hope with the New Year.
In nine months our year has gone almost full term.

The cold seas are grown almost warm enough for swimming,
The blue waters become brown and grey in autumnal light.
Yellow sunsets replace the orange of summer, the heat gone,
And slate sea mists drift into shore up Downland valleys.
A monochrome Weald awakes to September mornings,
Wood smoke curls from country cottages, bonfires scent the air.

In woodlands late-summer blooms still flower from hopeful buds,
Behind their Downland cousins, seeking the sun almost too late.
Early holly berries show, ready for Christmas picking, whilst
Rosehips, blackberries and nightshades peep through remaining hedgerows.
Nests vacated, birds consider moving on, save starlings and pigeons
In their city roosts, chattering loudly of take-aways and winter plans.

Featureless grey skies sometimes give way to Indian summers,
But, un-fooled, fungi cling to dead wood, spores exploded to disperse.
At night the air is heavy with the scents of wood, soil and plants.
The sky, filled with shooting stars, is clear and crisp, if unclouded.
September is the end of the beginning of the year and is the
Beginning of the end: Autumn equinox promising Beltane.

SHINE THIS DAY

There's a full moon over my house,
It finds an empty heart in my room.

There's such a silence in this night,
That it cries out in burning tears,

"Oh, Where is love?"

The golden sun will rise next dawn,
A silver moon beams on to my pillow,

My body will warm to its healing light,
But will I shine this day

Without that love?

WE'VE ALL BEEN THERE

Costa Brava, we've all been there.
Stratford, there as well
Westminster, there as well.

Home alone: we've all been there
Embraced by fear, there as well.
Alone again: we went that way.

Promised all: we've all been there.
Dumped, there as well.
Lost, out of love: we went that way.

SHOW ME

"Show me the man in the moon, my love."
"Where, oh where has he gone?"
"Show me the stars that shine bright this night."
"Why do you show me the sky?" "Show me the sun."
"It shines far too bright."

"Show me the love you showed me was right."
"Where, oh where has it gone?"
"Show me the love that you said you might."
"Why do you show me this lie?"
"Show me you'll stay, and won't go away."

"I'll show you the man in the moon, my love.
He's gone with a love that has passed.
I'll show you the stars that shone bright that night,
They stand far off in the sky.
I'll show you the sun, it burns far too bright."

"I'll show you the love that was right
Has gone. It's gone to another, you know.
I'll show you that love was right on the night.
Then, to me it was no lie. I'll not stay,
Our love has gone away."

"Show me that friends can be lovers, my love.
That lovers can also be friends."
"I'll show you that love can a friendship destroy,
Though friendship to love might well grow."
"Show me you'll wait, but I'll go away."

"Show me the happy ending, my love.
Why, oh why did you go? I just need a clue.
Show me the love we had was love that was true.
Oh why do you show me the door?"
"I'll show you no more, now you close that door."

SIXTIES PARTY

A party – a Sixties party:
Stilettos, tulip skirts, full petticoats,
Waspies, stockings - with
Plastic belt, plastic bag,
Beehive hairdos.
The men don't make much effort
The girls are better at it,
At the sixties look.

Few Teddy-boys,
Mods, Rockers,
Some old hippies.
But the music -
Beatles, Stones,
Simon and Garfunkel,
Buddy Holly, Bill Haley,
Comets!

We are teenagers again.
No reefers - it's pot now.
We start to jive:
Our children look amused,
Ask, "What was it really
Like in the old days?"
It was great, for we were
Young and groovy and hip!

Cuba Crisis, Berlin Wall,
Iron curtained our safety
Though we felt near to
World War Three.
The old Empire and
Europe exchanged roles
For New Elizabethans.

The excitement, CND
Marches, protests,
Radio Caroline, 45's,
Oh! The sixties!
But where is Kennedy now?

SOILED

Push it into me, plant your seeds well,
My flower covered bed is stirred by your
Strong hands and probing fingers.
I feel your sweat drip on to me.

I am not long out of the nursery,
Then I recall a green house, and
Now I lie thrown on the ground
Beaten almost flat under your weight.

Treated like all the rest, fertilised,
And walked on. You wield your tool
Like an expert. Were you born with
This garden spade in your hand?

Make your flowerbed and plant in it.
A flowerbed needs good soil, weeding
And plenty of compost, and a good deep
Dig through by the gardener to mix the soil.

SPACE AGE

Searching her words and her eyes,
I feel a need for confirmation.

We look the same; there are no others,
Tenderly our fingers touch.

Lovemaking feels more urgent,
Time never was on our side.

SPEEDING

She's speeding again.
    I do this too.

She won't slow down.
    We both grin.

She pretends I'm the learner
    When she drives.

Likes to be in the driving seat.
    But I'm held responsible

For her accidents.

SPRING SPRUNG

I lie, like a stone in mud, bedridden now.
Through my window I see springtime's bud,
Remember how spring is heralded first by
White … Snowdrops,
There is a progress of colours and of scents:
Yellow first, the crocus, forsythia and daffodil.
Later, wallflowers come in orange, reds, purples,
So many colours,

The hyacinth-blue night air drifts and sneaks in,
Heady with the scent from their aromatic,
Fine floppy flowers.
I know from the flower-pot in my room, and
From the garden outside which I cannot see,
That spring is sprung.

As a child, late spring walks were bluebell-shod.
How wretched they would seem two days later,
Dead in a vase,
Like my spirit.
The forget-me-not blues, even pinks these days,
Apple, pear, and cherry blossoms multiply,
They are too low to see,
From my bedroom window,

I just see the sky as Vincent did,
He at least could walk.
Forget not the old and the bed-bound
As you gather spring memories.
My sap no longer rises.
Pussy willow, catkin gatherer,
So go gather your
Spring branches.

My spring now sprung,
Like my old cat,
Who sits on my chest
Sometimes.

STARS MOVED ON

The light from the stars takes so long to reach us —
Light years, gone!

They have moved on, and are gone entirely.
Time's dimensions are lapsed by this distance.

A love that has ended may turn so sour in the mind —
Sad remembrance, lovers!

They have moved on, and are gone entirely.
This distance changes time's impressions.

The shooting stars, arcing across the void of space —
Burn to extinction!

They have moved on, and are gone entirely.
Time's brevity is clear through this distance.

The light of the sun, so bright, to warm us —
Our sunlit days!

They have moved on, and are gone entirely.
Time's change in life seen from this distance.

The light of the moon, so secret to steer us —
Brightens dark nights!

They have moved on, and are gone entirely.
Time's nights to days, a light in the distance.

STONE

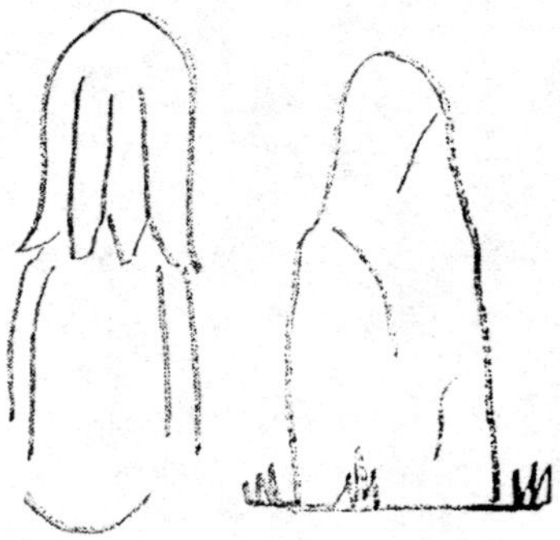

In her face I saw
The stone:

In the stone
I saw her face.

I carved the stone
To leave a monument
To the face I saw.

Life carved her face
To show the stone
Within her soul.

SUNRISE

Sunrise!
Surprise!
I saw her eyes!

How bright
The light
After our night!

The heat!
The treat!
So very neat!

Birds sing!
Bells ring!
Must be Spring!

We'll take it,
Wide awake it
Must be Love!!

STRICTLY FOR THE BIRDS

I knew a little duck
Who really liked to
Follow other birds

With glee he would honk
With geese he would bongo
Play loudly.

He had his little song
Which he sang, all day long,
"I love a great tit when I see one,

I like the occasional goose,
But best of all, in winter or fall,
What takes the bag,
Is a jolly good shag,
Ornithologically speaking
Of course."

This wicked drake,
No longer a rake,
Met a duck, named Meg.
Some days later, needless to say,
This duck had an egg,
And quacked,
"That was a jolly good lay."

STUDENT NURSE

First-night nerves on her first night-duty,
In charge of a chronic geriatric ward;
Twenty-four beds. Nobody had said, "Break a leg".
It is a different sort of theatre.

There was a tough parrot-nosed Sister in charge,
Roving to supervise two wards and
Their student nurse night-watchers, not enough trained staff
To be in either all night.

When starting duty there is "Report".
The previous shift recalls developments,
Things to watch, danger areas, duties,
Patients with special requirements.

"Pay particular attention to Mr Mason in bed 9, in the corner, he's very ill,
Ninety-seven, very frail, all his systems are failing; he's just for "TLC".

When his breathing gets irregular and laboured it means he is expected to
Die very soon, pull the curtains and call sister. Do not try to resuscitate".

At about four in the morning, sure enough from bed 9 there was that gasping,
Terrible, irregular breathing. Quietly nurse closed the curtains and got sister.

It's Mr Mason, he's going," she whispered. Sister went behind the curtains
And quickly returned. "He's not going, he's coming! He's masturbating!

A nurse who does not know the difference between coming and going
Has a few things to learn!"

TLC is a nursing expression for Tender Loving Care, i.e. no serious interventions.

SUSSEX FLINT CHURCH

** Lullington, near Alfriston*

Sussex flint church; shrunk with passing time;
Congregation dwindled, graveyard full: a quiet place.
Oaks and yew trees encircle it; untidy hedges are its walls.
No grave is recent, no bouquets, but wild flowers grow
Here. The door is unlocked. We go through.
One service a month. There are few visitors.
Inside it is whitewashed; has patches of green damp;
Smells of mould, wood-wormed timbers and cold stone.
Light filters through dirty clear glass windows,
Some cracked; rays of warmth in catacomb cold.
We walk there like pilgrims, stand alone, or
Wander like moths, whispering in wonder

At the work of centuries time-capsuled here
In this once central, now edge-of-the-village building.
A simple cross at the altar. Colour given by
Week-old flowers in Norman arch framed focus.
The floor lay, gravestone lined, forgotten beneath
Our feet, over the bones of squires and villagers.
Together in this, the smallest church in Sussex,
Alive in this redundant place, at that moment it was ours.
We signed the book. The last wedding had been
Two years before. I felt the warmth of your skin,
Smelt your perfume. Your presence there delighted me.
I felt happy, at ease, until I saw your face show boredom.

Outside again; on tumulus tump - the graveyard,
Where the Christian church stood against its Druidic
Predecessor, you said you sensed the history in the soil,
Felt the force I have known so long in this holy place.
I crossed the bone yard, felt the cold shadow of another
Walk over my grave, felt the fear of losing your love.
I saw distraction on your forehead; saw your smile
Had gone. In spirit you were with someone else.
Long after we have parted and died, this little church
Will witness the coming and going of lovers,
Of life and death: and wild flowers will surely
Grow each spring in the burial ground.

TAKE A GENTLE HAND

I miss her each day as though it was a thousand years.
I remember too much and wonder if she thinks of our time?
She was quite unique. I'm glad to have held her, to know
What love could be and hope she's found that love.

A love that's held back can be a life's greatest pain,
I say love another, love again and wish her only well.
Time to take a gentle hand, to come or go, even forever,
To just remember she was and is so loved, and still by me.

I am perhaps the moon to the light of her sun and may only
Truly shine in that, now gone, but oh so bright a light.

THE CIRCLE

From the centre of my world to beyond the edge,
From deep in my soul to slip into dreams, our
Shared life has ended leaving only joyful past.
Our parting, an agony to be buried and forgotten.

The sun closed his eyes, left me with a heat-full loss,
The hateful moon watched my weeping lost wishes.
You are gone and now I ache in remembrances.
I am alone, real friends show care and concern.

Was our love a dream? Did you love too?
Was it real for you? Do you forget the joy?
I feel you are mistaken, have changed to an unknown.
I fear you have left one imperfection for another.

Something new is not always something better.
Something in someone else cannot kill the good.
There is nothing to forgive, but much to forget.
There is no way to explain why another stops caring.

How then can I pretend to hate, to learn to detach?
Will I ever forget the dream of love or find its match?
The circle of living and dying, loving and going.
The circle that will never end.

TAROT

Queen of Swords, covered by King of Wands;
Her friend Queen of Cups displaced, face torn.
The Wheel of Fortune turned, after the Enchantress
Spurned her. She sought Two of Cups yet again

The Tower lay close, the Hanged Man un-reversed,
Lovers come and go; Swords and Wands prevail.
Cups and Coins excite, as do Twos and Fives; yet
Destiny throws the deck; interpretations are personal.

Justice, Pope, and Empress, Joker crowd: powerful cards.
A year displayed in a hand, present situation focussed.
The full picture in other decks, the one theme is self.
Castles of cards, patterns on paper, fate lives dispensing.

Lies or Truths, Lovers touched by the Magician.
Fate - the Three of Wands is omnipotent, even the
Devil subdued, Sunshines through Death, again.
Shuffle, place left handed, choose. Don't talk about it.

Pray well before arranging the Spread, carefully -
You hold all the cards; solutions found if you seek them:
With meditation and perspective a creative answer shows.
Guide the mind to understanding, not playing at life.

THE BRICK WALL

Cement bag, so heavy to carry,
Is dragged by me from the car
To the shed. Grey powder covers
My dress; that dry quicklime smell.

Bricks stand neat and in pairs,
Alternately at right angles, like
My child's building blocks. These
Are expensive red engineering bricks.

A string and skewer with a spirit level
Made by me at school, gives me my line.
Foundation already dug, I start to mix mortar.
Cheerful thoughts of mud pies, sandcastles.

It is hard work mixing this satisfying grey
Sludge sliced and folded on the shovel.
With trowel I slop it along the base line,
And pat it into place. I lay the bricks.

Neatly I finish each one as I go, level,
Point and tap into place one by one.
You can lay five bricks high before it goes off
And becomes unstable. This wall will outlast me.

With a 1989 coin buried under my wall,
I sign my initials in the cement.
My solid graffiti for my grandchildren
To see, Grannie built that wall.

THE CHILD

A child in me said "Believe",
I believed the child in me.
Look", she said, "Look and see"
I looked and saw your eyes.

The child in you smiled on me,
We each believed in that child.
"Love", we said, please love me.
We loved and asked no "Why's"

THE POPPY

She was collecting
For Charity.

Charity is love.
I gave all I could:
All of myself;
And was left
With nothing
When she went away

I search now for a
Collector's tin

To replace the lead
In my soul,
So its gold could
Shine again.
I wear the red poppy:

Remember, but
Try to forget

THE CRADLE

Red ochre stained in a holy place,
By a woman with soil; made from the
Creator's dry blood in the
Dreamtimes.

This cradle; light, delicate, curved,
Part fashioned by its maker from a broken
Eucalyptus branch

Part accidentally by witchetty grubs,
Part using a Marsupial's tooth,

Made to carry her baby,
Berries, or water.

Those with so few possessions have only
Such utterly practical and
Beautiful things:

More personal than anything
We may have.

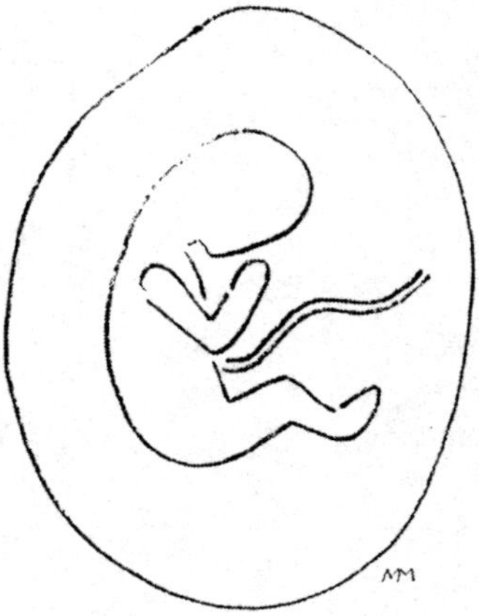

THE DOG LOVER

My dear friend is looking for a lover.
She must be gentle, slim, available,
Intelligent: And a dog lover.

He met such a woman … Delighted,
Was invited to her home for dinner.
It grew late, they gelled …

She asked him if he would like to stay.
"Yes please" he replied, knowing she
Only had one bed, a new one at that...

Naked in each other's arms on the bed,
Passions rising … He glimpsed an object
Lift like a Harrier Jet from the ground,
Hurtle towards them and land between them.

The Airborne Dog collapsed the bed.
All fell in a tangle, all passion gone.

Dazed, the trio stared at each other in disbelief.
The dog licked their faces apologetically.
They slept in celibacy on the floor.

THE DRAGONFLY

** An October afternoon, sunshine between showers, the algae encrusted chalk rubble was bound together with brambles, rain-washed blackberries glowed in the sunlight. Wild elderberries and rosehips reminded me of homemade wines and jams. A large green dragonfly alighted on a stone near my hand, unaware that I watched her while I rested from my search for fossils. As her wings quivered in the warming light, it reminded me of an afternoon spent by a lake in Hampstead. A time when I was very alone, felt very down in the dumps. It reminded me of when such a dragonfly climbed a reed's stem out of the water, dragging her caddis cocoon behind her.*

I had placed my finger above her and she had climbed onto it.
Now, finally releasing herself from her aquatic past life,
Her crumpled wing-buds were draped along her slender back.
I marvelled at the urgent way her lifeblood force filled them,
Visibly growing, extending, until they reached her long tail's ending.
One by one her wings moved gently from her sides, unfurled and dried.
Wings, which though transparent released rainbow patterns which danced
As they quivered and trembled their excitement of form and growing strength.
She was testing them as they hardened and gained their full extent.

This done she seemed somehow heavier and more
Formidable, but this dragonfly remained on my hand
So still, until she was satisfied all was right.
How did she know, who taught her to fly?
Her metamorphosis, her life, almost complete.
How did she not feel fearful, or joyful or amazed?
Still and silently I watched this little miracle.
The extraordinary is mundane in Nature.
Remember you only need take time to see,
To experience, to be a part of it, to simply be.

Time moved slowly by, she walked to my fingertip and started to fly,
Her iridescent emerald body flashed above the calm pool's water
Wherein she had spent the largest and first part of her life.
The flight's freedom was meant to be, was her destiny.
She had not realised I had shared that critical time with her,
No bird preyed on her, now she was gone, searching for a mate.
My mood was changed utterly, she taught me something about moving on,
About freedom, about beauty and wonder, about learning to stop and
Truly experience something, not to rush, to feel the warmth of the sun,
Extending, growing and trusting in a future, about life force.
Now, years on, another dragonfly is also close to me with those
So large compound eyes, and wonderful jewel wings.

THE FLOWERS OF THE FOREST

Willow branches curve to form a
Cathedral canopy of weeping leaves:

Lilac and rosemary for remembrance,
Leaves dust the aromatic air.

Honesty, purple flowered, paper-disc
Seedpods disperse the memory.

Yellow-blossomed broom's blemished brown
Spikes of deep green sweep the wind.

Thyme waits for no woman, and the
Wild rose's tangle taunts us

With their so delicate petals, which struggle for
Sunlight against sharp bramble weeds.

They tell of the passing of the season
And of ageing for no reason.

Tears watered my woodland.
This wind of change has broken

The strong trunk of the oldest tree:
The tree of Love. It slowly rots.

Fungi thrive on decay:
Leaves and flowers lie crushed,

Yet bright new buds may
Form from old ground

When winter's gone.

THE GAZEBO

There's a gazebo at the bottom of my garden,
Where I once sat with my lover reading poems,
Where we ate secret meals alone together.
Where, at parties, a few and a bottle would settle.

There's a wooden Wendy house of a building,
I put up from a bargain kit, brought in a sale,
Filled with chairs and a table with a Singer
Sewing machine base and homemade pine tabletop.

Tongued and grooved - it's groovy, a place away;
To be private, conspiratorial, childlike, secreted.
Secretive. Pretentiously, it looks out on my little
Garden and too fast fills with wine fumes and smoke.

The glazed double doors draw open like opening arms
And close like my own Tardis, without control buttons.
It smells of wood, and wine and varnish and mud,
It warms quickly when we cram in to eat breakfast.

Yes, there's a gazebo at the bottom of my garden.
It's my folly, but it's private, waterproof and sound.
"Bring some Rioja, I'll get an ash tray, plates,
And some home baked apple crumble. You should see it."

THE GIFT

Beautifully wrapped, with red ribbon.
Carefully tied, around its mysterious
Shape.

A rectangular form, heavy, it rattled when lifted,
Gave no clue of its
Contents.

Paper and tape drawn back, it opened
To careful fingers. The box lay revealed, to
Open.

The lid lifted; longingly she peered inside,
A swarm of flying things flew out to her world,
Free.

The girl was delighted,
Caught some in her
Hands.

They were beauteous,
But consumed
Pandora.

She had become an adult.

THE GOOD LAND

The white men came with their guns,
They took to themselves the lands.
They brought with them wire fences,
So my cattle could not graze
On the good land.

Traders came, and took ivory,
When they could no longer take us
As slaves. With them, came chains,
So my people were taken away
From the good land.

White hunters came, slaughtered the game,
Leaving to rot what we might eat.
They brought cameras with them,
That they might photograph us
On the good land.

New leaders came, we were free.
They took our ancestral lands.
They were from other tribes,
We voted for them with our mark
Of the good land.

Modern times came, by air, in trucks,
On foot, with movie cameras.
THEY were still white, like the ivory
They wanted to make trinkets
From the good land.

Elephant and rhinoceros we hunted
With our arrows, and our guns.
THEY shoot US, for game is protected.
They wish to drive us forever
From the good land.

THE HOUSE OF MEMORIES

The house of memories, where something dwells,
Remaining between one's truth and another's:
Where such rooms are filled with events seen
From different perspectives; so they become
As different events, with different players;
In the parts we led, and followed, and lived.
In this house it depends who writes the play
And how it is read and who listens, or hears,
And when the story is told, even to oneself.

"Those were good times", one says, sentimentally.
The other, "I was unhappy then", seeing only her truth.
"I remember the moonlight"; she saw the moon.
"It was dark that night"; the other remembers, for
She only saw darkness that night. Nights are dark.
Each looks so closely for what she sought or needed
Or wanted from that night, that she neglects to be
Objective: for if love's lost, all's seen subjectively:
So, feelings obscure the facts, and that light is lost.

In love the object becomes a light to fill the mind
And memory: so light, it renders past love so grey
That it is lost; past attractions soon outweighed
By present distractions, reactions and then actions.
So why do we run from the past, or mourn the passing,
For it was a different past for each of us, when seen
From changed emotions, when felt with altered devotions?
But our present is built on the shifting, uncertain,
Unsteady foundation of such a house of mobile memory.

THE HOUSE YOU DRAW

Draw a box with a dark line. In the centre along the base, put in a vertical
Oblong only half the height of the square, with smaller squares either side
And in line, each divided by a cross, three similar symmetrical squares
Placed in line above them.

Above and joined to this square box by its longest side; a large triangle,
From which vertically projects a tiny thin oblong to the right,
Coming upward from the angle, sides almost parallel to the page,
Like the straight sides of large square. From its top, lines like smoke
Curl up the page, set side-less, two dimensional on that page,

Your house needs a garden, trees, surroundings and on the paper-sky above
A circle-sun, with yellow-line rays to all quarters and the house,
Perhaps, too, a squiggly bird captured in stillness, winging across the
White of the page above the house. Some small cotton-wool clouds on a
Painted blue sky with green fields to the page's middle to meet that sky.
The door will be red, or blue, or green to open, but stays shut. Inside is secret,
A mystery; closed for each of the small square windows reflects nothing,
And stares out white. We wonder what lies behind them?

This house has no back. Its windows stay shut.
It is silent, private, comfortable and strong.
Perhaps you will draw a wall or fence around it,
With a closed gate to the garden and front.
Then that garden will have flowers, big as trees,
And frying-pan flat-shaped green topped trees,
With brown vertical trunks, and neat angled branches,
Not a single leaf out of place.

In front the grey road goes horizontally
From left to right, from nowhere to anywhere.
There might be a car parked outside,
The two facing wheel-circles shown, the others
Hidden behind in the paper, Like so much else.
Matchstick people might be in the garden or road.
There is no perspective, no prospect in such a house.
Where is the real house of children and of dreams?
This house stands in the middle of the page, alone,
Its view is of the viewer, the house opposite, its eyes.
All these lines are closed, right angled and balanced.
Draw closer and consider how you might draw your house.

THE IVORY TOWER

She shut her care in a stone turret, remote and safe
In mountain isolation, watched people, observing
From above, their hands held together, tied
In their sun-filled happy valley.

She played chess with their lives,
Not comprehending their views,
Then cut them dead and left.
The Ivory tower was her observation post.

She dreamt of a man on an identical peak,
Span a golden rope ladder with her hair,
Tendrils steady held fast to climb, or to cut,
Lowered it down to the valley of a life vacated.

Knowing what to do with the ladder
She provided, blindly he climbed,
Though a gulf remained, for her tower
Still stood strong against others.

Using such ladders could be useful employment,
She could always remove the supports.
However strong the builder or climber,
She knew what proximity to another might do.

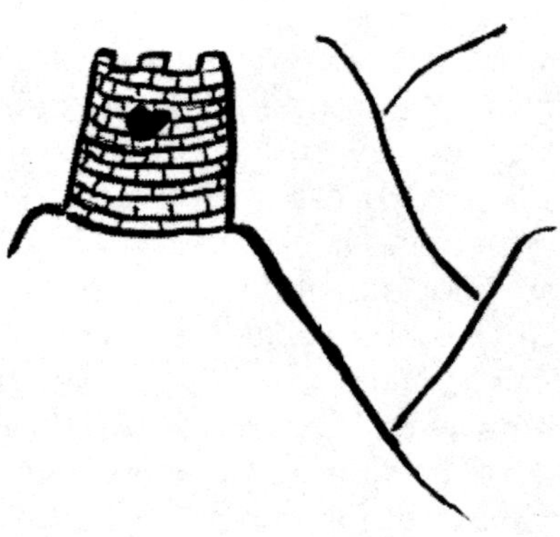

THE LOCAL PLAYERS

A friend and I went to see the local players.
"I remember Mama", a weepy.
Most of the audience on that the second night
Had zimmered their way to the theatre hall.
Rep' wrapped at its best banality.
There were two shows. One, excellent, on stage,
The other in the row in front of us.
A trio of old widows.
The fattest and youngest in the middle.
She had a faded plastic flower in her dyed hair.
On her left, part sighted, part deaf, ninety,
On her right still as death, a corpse like crone
Sat silently. Perhaps she died before the show
Or had been there since the previous performance.
Fat lady talked of the young men she fancied,
Her older companion had stopped hoping or seeing.
The play began. "That's's 'er, ain't she luvley?" Our
Commentator talked on, delighted each time she
She saw a woman she thought she knew in the play.
The interval came. Sticks and frames clicked into
Action. A race for the 30p cuppa and biscuits.
Thin lady asked fat lady,
"Who's the man you come with?"

Fat lady turned to look at him.
"That ain't a man it's me son".
He shuffled nervously after
Fifty years a mother's boy.
"Who's the man beside 'im?"
"That ain't a man it's a lady"
They both stared at the shorthaired
Woman in the aisle seat.
In a world of their own the elderly
Have realities, which are so different,
And of little consequence. Just like the play.
Jumble sales and bingo and a night out matter
This was their big night out, a treat.
It was real theatre.

The dead lady hurried out past us as we left.

THE OLD FRIEND

An old friend held tightly,
Our arms entwined, standing
Together, eyes speaking care.

We have been through much,
Only truth told to each other,
The way lovers rarely do.

There is no idealism in this love:
No false concepts, no need
For either to change

Or adapt to please the other.
Each has listened, tried to help,
Laughed, tried not to cry.

Such friends are rare.
We know so many people,
Very few are true friends.

THE PUNT

★on holiday in Central France

Lying alone, face over the prow of a punt on the
River Allier; in a quiet side-water, three metres deep
And clear; so clear sun's rays pointed to the bottom –
I saw a long, log like, grey-green shape, move slowly.

He saw me, this pike. We purposely drifted
In the sun's light heat, watching one another,
A joining of space, two worlds, his and mine,
I glimpsed the wonder of his private place.

The wind ruffled my short summer skirt.
I let my fingers dangle through the water's
Surface. He let small fish play near his
Great gaping toothed jaws, unconcerned.

My hair fell about my face, framing its
Reflection and dangling in the clear water,
Just as the weeds reached up to the light
From below, green and golden tendrils to
Join our worlds; too hot and lazy to move.

I wonder if he too recalls that moment?

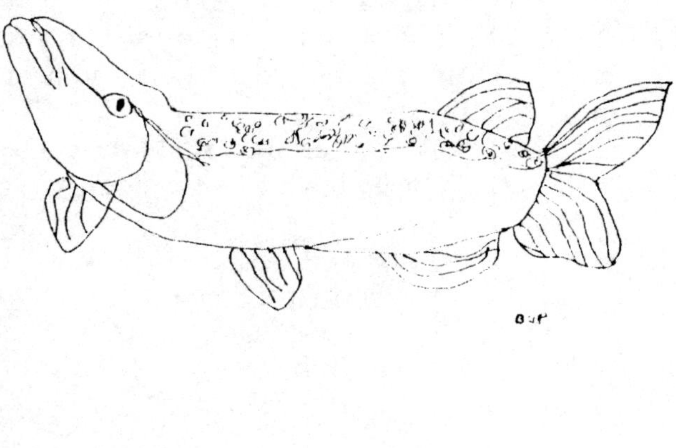

THE SMALL STONE

At the end of my flower filled field of love
A small stone appeared and began to grow.
Unseen by me, stealthily placed by another,
This stone, grey hard, lay hidden, obscured
Beneath our petals of pink, red and white,
Our meadows of memories.

Unnoticed, it grew daily, to a rising rigid rock:
Outlived the summer season of our flowers.

By winter it obscured the Sun, hid the light.
It grew dark, this heart shaped mountain menace,
Ice capped, bleak, black, un-climbable barrier.
It grew so tall I had to walk round it to see it.
A tiny stone to the next lover, a crushing rock to me.
I prayed for a sort of friendship to survive,

Perhaps that seed might root near this jagged rock,
Which now closed her heart to my hope.

I tried to grow that seed strong, so to bloom again,
Only it was impossible to switch off this cruel love.
My resistance could not allow love to transform,
To gain love's destruction by using healing hate.
A life-long love outlives any anger or hate.

At first I found a stone in that seed had grown
So great it almost died, as had my hope of love.
Only the healing waters of time would slowly
Let that seed grow again, and grind such stones to dust.

My love had become a stone, making
A friendship hard for us both

Time gave a chance to move away
From that Stone,
To see again,
To be again,
My friend

THE TREE AND I

★ *Written for my eldest daughter soon after the birth of my first grandchild*

Sycamore leaves lie piled high across my path.
I planted it the day of my First-born's Birth,
It has recognised its twenty-fourth autumn,
And stands naked against the winter.

Lawn-sown helicoptered seeds of last year
Lie dormant; flowerbeds sport young saplings.
Seedlings creep through cracks in paving stones,
Even though winter is just round the corner.

Dark slugs graze lazily on rotting wetness,
Whilst the soil smells sweetly of decay.
I have stopped bonfiring the old leaves,
I rake and pile them high to compost.

Many wind-born leaves move back up the path
Into the kitchen, where the cat plays with one,
Forgetting his dignity, he is no longer a kitten,
As an adult he can't be seen at play.

I stare at the tree and remember I must soon
Start to be grownup, for now I'm a Grannie.
Older and a little wiser, I learnt to understand.
Even after a hurricane that tree could still stand.

The tree's lichen-stained bark, like my face,
Shows signs time, of ageing in cracks and lines.
Its twigs sway skywards gently in the breeze,
As my fingers brush crumbs from my dress.

My fingers are thinner and weaker, now can do less.
Sometimes I would put my arms around that tree
And remember how little my daughter used to be:
How she has grown up, is well grounded, like me.

★ *To dear Rebecca.*

THE WOMAN I WAS TO BE

As a child I starred into the mirror
To see the woman I was to be.

I danced quietly alone, looking at
Other more beautiful girls, with joy
At their great good fortune.

I hated my body; so cultivated my mind;
My soul showed through my careful words
And considerations.

My parents did not understand each other,
Or me; parted and talked only of themselves.

Marriage, lovers, ideals, gave but a
Glimpse of that dream of being loved.

A woman who loves other women, and
Regards men as equals,

Almost.

THE WOMAN ON MY LEFT

Nearly Easter, Christmas Cards
Still up weeks after the event.

Pine needles on the floor,
Sagging bladder-dead balloons
Hang sadly on a picture.

The fire was lit with bits of
Wood and rubbish and coal.

People are coming.
The house puts its face on.
A house needs people,
Not one alone.

Best china out, dishes on table,
She gives her orders.
I try to help, get it wrong,
It's got to be done her way.

They arrive; She's all fun and
Cuddles, witty and warm.
Sits with me sometimes,

On stage again;
Laughs at her guests
And hugs others;

Her teasing sexuality.
I long for the quiet bath
Together, the last cup of tea,

The woman on my left.

THERE ARE FERRIES AT THE BOTTOM OF MY GARDEN

It is Christmas on the cross channel ferry.
My friends and I see the tree high on the mast.
Coloured lights hang in the rigging.
Day-trippers have last-minute's Christmas
Gifts wrapped in France, made in England,
To take home to loved ones.

A French Father Christmas greeted us
With "Joyeuse Noel" in the garlic
Scented air of cold Dieppe.
It drizzled, just like home, in the
Polite provincial French streets.
Shopping is less frenetic in French.
"Toujours la politesse", gift wrapped with love.

Little time in France, too long at sea
From Newhaven to Dieppe, but calm.
European voices murmur in Gitanne mists
In the bar. The coffee is good, laced with brandy.
Engine turns gently, lulling us to sleep.
A French yawn is much like an English.

My old Renault awaits us in the car park,
If we get by Customs with our extra Duty-free.
Groups of women, on this girls' day out,
Slowly sink in wine filled drowsiness.
We resolve to go together again.
"The restaurant will close in 30 minutes"

Once film, shopping, exploring the ship
Are done, the journey is too long a trip.
A routine, crossing to our island again.
From Dieppe, seems little distance to Kiev.
To go home we had to cross England's moat,
Which held back Hitler and Napoleon.
We travelled for five pounds on this boat.

Day trippers, tripped down gang planks,
Plastic bagged wine, cheese, perfume, and cigs
Clutched nervously through the green channel.
Grateful to be on English soil, we climb
Into the car, to drive on the left.
Right for the continent,
Hove for the incontinent.

THISTLE DOWN

Autumn too soon,
Old man's beard,

Whisper of wool on wire,
Cotton grass blown, grey.

A grey eyebrow hair.
Spring aches to return.

Season of shooting stars,
Falling from the firmament:

Of leaves licked by the winds,
Flying in clouds across roads.

Hats pulled over heads of hair,
Which whips about the face.

Seventh Roman month, summer's end.
Helicoptered sycamore seeds, acorns,

Plane leaves crisp and brittle.
A golden time, autumnal log fires,

Bonfire smoke sparks skywards,
Wet leaves heaped by a tidy wind.

Crackle of twigs underfoot, fungi.
Creak of ageing bones feeling the chill.

Crops taken in, heavy harvest-time.
Sloe gin, rosehip jelly, sticky jam.

Time to harvest our memories, nearer now,
Ready for the winter of our lives.

TIME GENTLEMEN

Time gentlemen please.
It is time for the women
To stop wars over territory,
Men's wealth and power.

Time to let the kind grow
For equality, not emulating
The males to gain power.

Women beware women
Who woo wealth and force.
No strength is greater than love.

UNDERSTANDING

"I'm just putting my face on", she said.
She wore no make-up, just a face she put on.
"Let's dress for dinner", he said.
It might be more fun to undress.
"I think I've caught a cold", he said
But he'd missed the boat, and
Dropped too many clangers.
"I've a headache," she said,
Meaning her heart ached,
For she felt so alone with him now.
"I love you ", he said, knowing he wanted sex.
"I want to make love to you" – meaning "at you."
She talked so long he could no longer hear,
He didn't listen, long until she was asleep, childlike.
He lay beside her, beside himself.
He didn't understand women
Because they understood him.

TO BE

To sink gently into your own bed,

To sit confidently on your own loo.

To eat when you wish, what you can afford,

To keep your bowels closed for a day,

To have no drips, no tubes, no charts,

To wear your own nightie, which fits,

To have junk on, around and under your bed,

To deliberately disobey doctor's orders,

To put the light on and off yourself.

To abandon diets and good intentions;

To blow your nose on a handkerchief;

To sit at a table to dine, and drink wine.

To escape the all-powerful tea-lady's trolley,

To dress in one's own clothes, not be expected

To undress to allow students to stare, to inspect.

To be out of hospital again, even if it does seem

To be a very long time getting better.

TO LIE

There is power in a lie,
So lie with me,

Lie to me,
Lie of me.

Truth lies deeper than lies.
Truth is relative.

Relatives lie,
But not with each other;
Though often to each other.

Look at the lie of the land.
The lie of the land.

Not enough to go round.
So many lie abed.

Lies are flat
So lie flat
And think of England.

TREE FERN

In a shady part of the woodland jungle it stands alone,
All of five metres tall, giant fronds spill from its crown.
It shouldn't grow here in Ireland, but does, warmed by
The Gulf Stream, in it's own temperate rain forest.
It is about two hundred years old, brought here by a
Collector, from its native New Zealand.

An old land where mankind did not trouble nature
Until a thousand years ago when the Maoris arrived.
They used its fronds as night markers to point their way
In the moonlight, the silver undersides reflect moonshine:
Each element of the frond mimics the whole,
It is a tiny fractal of the whole plant.

Magnified it resembles it so exactly.
A double row of seeds attached under each frond
Shows it is not a tree, as do the brown coils of new growth.
If you see a tree alone uncut, unmanaged, by man,
You will see that its outline shape often
Is the same shape as one of its leaves.

This fern is a living fossil, it and the Monkey Puzzle
Has grown in this way from the time of the dinosaurs.
Forests of tree ferns covered Pangea, the super continent
That included Antarctica. Its fossils lie so deep under the ice.
In Coal Measures if you split the clay you may find perfectly
Preserved leaves of tree ferns and club mosses.

Yet in this place you may stand in the same shade
As the great reptiles, though they are long gone.
I wonder what living fossil may remain
When we are also extinct,
Thanks to Global Warming,
Greenhouse Effect or Nuclear Winters?

VIDEO LIFE

If life were a video recorder
I'd record only good bits,
And erase or leave out the bad.
I'd stop screen violence.
I'd fast forward the bores,
And the materialist advertisers
I'd keep tape after tape of you.

If life were a video camera
I'd film beauty and nature,
I'd edit away the dross,
And zoom in on our love.
I'd soft-focus life's blemishes,
Faults in human nature.
I'd record all your moods.

If life were a video tape
I'd play it again and again,
And replay for a happy childhood.
I'd keep my parents happy together,
I'd ensure that love was forever.
I'd see that God was really kind,
Always answering good prayers.
I'd wipe out ageing and illness.

If life were a video film
I'd not buy images of power-mad politicians,
I'd hire only free thoughts
I'd marvel at life.
I'd show it to you,
Knowing you love goodness.
I'd see only Justice on Earth.

If life were a video-life I'd fill it to the full.
The good or the bad,
I'd learn from my mistakes.
I'd not feel erased,
I'd not be depressed.
Drinking life's gift joyfully, undaunted,
Un-haunted by your having gone.

WASPS

Old hollow logs drying, piled by the wall outside, to carve, or burn next winter.
Placed there to season in the sun: these amputated spurs of a now dead tree.
A bonfire nearby had disturbed them; only a few at first, then a great
Kamikaze Buzz, a cloud of angry yellow and black fighting creatures.

Selfless, they defend their queen, the grubs, the nest, their home.
Fearful, I know they must go. They are too near the window,
May swarm indoors and harm us. Carefully I approach them
With the hosepipe spraying a protecting wall of water.

Wet, they fall to the ground, stunned. The beauteous cone is exposed,
The delicate cellulose matrix of their symmetric design shatters,
Wriggling white grubs are washed out with that stream,
Suicidal workers risk all, rush in, and try to save them.

Sensing the danger, the destruction, they swarm, an angry cloud of
Stinging sisters, stings filled with Formic acid seeking this intruder.
My gloved hand lifts the logs, clears the nest, dropping it into a bucket of water.
The large queen floats out, drowning.

Two days later surviving dispossessed workers
Still search for grubs, and new home.
But wasps recover; surely some will find
More suitable accommodation.
I feel guilty at their distress,
But glad they are gone.

WERE THEY WATCHING?

Was anyone watching as I sat on the swing?
Did they see me dance by moonlight in the park?
Could they guess at fifty I still like playgrounds?
It's better now I'm supposed to be grownup,
Nobody fusses that it might be dangerous hanging from the high bars
By hands not used to hold me up.
Did they laugh as I walked in the puddle, splashes up my legs?
That exquisite liberation and Deliberation as I enjoy the water, mud and
The sloshing squelch of wellington boots full of water:
Then I lean forward, knee bent, leg behind to let it run out,
Like from a teapot spout. I laugh at the slimy discomfort of wet stockings and feet.
Do they guess I rush deliberately into piles of golden autumn leaves?
I whish them with my feet, then tidy them with the sides of my boots,
Satisfied with the high heap for winds to lick, whilst wishing they were dry that
I might lie there in them, a would-be babe in the woods,
To listen to the gentle silence of the countryside and to my heart's beat.
Can they guess the joy of burying legs in soft shingle on the beach?
Leaving just a toe to peep out, as though it wasn't mine, to be my easy
Target for small stones?
Do they remember how good it is to bounce a pebble on the waves,
To beach comb and collect pretty stones?
Have they never thought that they too are still children?
The child in us lives on; still, small, and so quiet voiced.
But so often she's frightened or lonely she cannot speak.
With beaches, puddles, leaves, mud, water and wind and woodlands,
Who can resist throwing her arms round an old tree, touched by its age and size,
Its new buds and life?
Why don't judges and policemen, vicars and nuns and mums play in the park?
Why do we feel so self-conscious at our childlike joy in life and nature?
Give in to what's natural!
The most self-imaged old cat still chases imagined mice in his dreams.
My old dog still knows how to play with a stick.
See a dog rolling in cow's muck? Well, perhaps that's not for me.

It's not done for grown-ups to be themselves, or even for many children.
We are to be seen and not heard, to behave, sit properly, be good, act our age.
If people leapfrogged in Tesco's, wouldn't it be fun waiting for the till girl to
Check our trolleys? But we'd be thought, off our trolleys.
As I stood in the snow, licking an ice-cream, who cares if
They were they watching?

WHY?

First the sniper - an old wound opened;
Then the minefield - dangerous to talk of important things;
Now the barrage - reproaches.
And the attack - "how could you?"
Meets retaliation - a counter attack.
A marriage ended - a lawyer's delight

The field is covered in mines -

A skylark wings and sings high above. - The shells are silent now

The bodies of the lovers lie in contortions of pain
- Joined in tragedy, foes fingers touch.

The wounded are carried off, - The dead buried in this
common grave.

An unknown warrior of the Great War, - Sides don't matter now.

We will remember them - And do it again.

A field covered in wild flowers, the harvest gathered in for another year.
An overgrown trench, bunkers, rusting shrapnel, shell holes scar this landscape.
A war grave, memorial in the sun.

A broken home, a fight for children. - Things and feelings are fought over.
Lovers, politicians, generals, children, - All as one cut down peace for an idea,

Arms dealers, lawyers and estate agents are the beneficiaries.

We see the waste and people ask

"Why?"

WHY ME?

"Why me?" I ask, having put down the 'phone,
After yet another person has asked for my advice,
Which they will probably, quite sensibly, ignore.
Even I do not follow my own considered thoughts.
I always act from the heart, which utterly rules my head.

"Why me?" A question often put to me, by others who have
Suffered life's pain, injustices, hardships and blows,
They share this with me, though I am powerless to change
Things for them, as I might wish, to make things right.
How often that magic wand might have helped us both.

"Why me?" I ask myself, an Earth Mother, well grounded,
Well rounded: Who is expected to understand and listen,
Who suffers much herself, but finds sharing her own pain
Quite difficult. Indeed, type-cast as a good listener has so
Often denied me the ability or time to unburden myself.

"Why me?" I think as I stare into the mirror at lines life
Has left on my face; I see middle age, but inside a clumsy
Girl still rushes about with the joyful haphazard optimism
Of never-quite-lost teenage ideals or dreams or sense of fun,
Whose body makes it less easy to be her carefree inner self.

"Why me?" I write, reflecting at the mistaken privilege of
Being thought wise, which nursing and living has given me.
Wisdom may have grown through my own experience, and others'
Words. They do at least help me to find common factors in our
Pain and lets them ask me, even rhetorically, "Why me?"

WISDOM

We sat side by side
My ex-lover and I.

We dared not touch.
My words were of poems:

So much unfinished business
Un-said, unsure, unsafe,

Un-united, we were at least
Polite at last.

I went to my home,
Felt better for it.

Learning to be a stranger
Is so very strange:

Not to ask obvious questions:
Not to expect honest answers.

She looked a bit spotty
I looked much older.

Neither of us was wiser
When we parted

WRITING IN THE CLAY

In Sumeria Eridoo lies,
The world's first city,
Seven millennia old.
It was they, the Sumerians,
Who divided time and space
Into parts of sixty.

The epic tale of Gilgamesh
Was the world's first story.
It was he, who built the walls,
He sought everlasting life
Before the Bible was written.
Words, as deeds, were his monuments.

His story was written in a script we
Can read and understand today; it,
Like ours, tells a story without the speaker,
Unlike ours, was made by wooden wedge marks,
Made in soft clay by scribes, as a fixed key,
A record, a reference to memory and knowledge.

Writing was first found here in a book.
Accounts were kept, stories told, drawn.
Lineages preserved for all time, when their
Bones had long gone. They left us these words,
"To a far off day in a far off time,
On a far off night". It is written still.

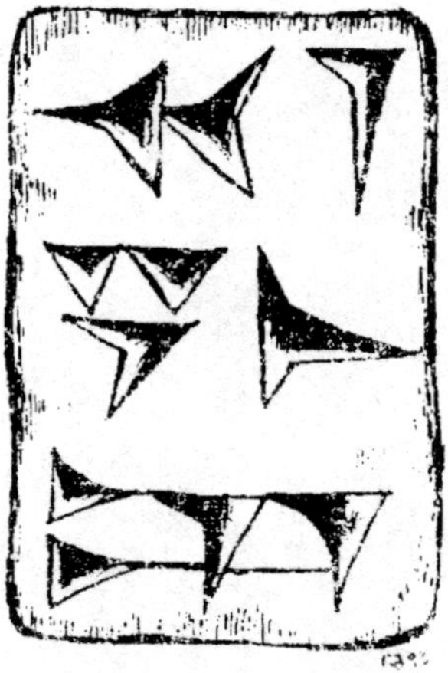

YOU CAME UNEXPECTED

Walled into a tomb of cold black stone,
Unable to love, a hard rock protected me.
Beyond, lovers could dance in the sun
As once I danced to my empty place.
Un-espoused, love gone without a trace.
Pain built that wall, which was destroyed,
You were the only one with that light to change
The obsidian despair to diamonds, catacomb to palace.
New life grew in the strength of days and laughter,
And nights shared, nightmares stayed undreamed.
You came unexpected, that so welcome guest
Bearing the cup we shared, and I seek now.
The gifts of honesty, youth, beauty and hope
Were ours to explore, to become builders,
Learning each other, explorers, sharing our loads.

You came, unexpected,
    A snowdrop through snow.
    An iridescent fish in deep waters.
    A green flame in a fire.
    A newborn baby's smile.
    A laughing girl with golden hair.
You came and were wanted
    Like the first breath of air.
    Like a log fire in winter,
    A spinning top on a table
    A wish on birthday candles
    Someone to give my all.

You came and lit fires
    In my heart, in my soul.
    In my eyes, in my body.
    You shared all my desires.
    You burnt all others from me.
    Your beacon still burns bright.
You came and were kind.
    You shared all of your fear.
    You gave me joy and youth.
    You lavished your time.
    You showed me I could be loved.
And you left, unexpected.

ZEBRA CROSSING

In the black dark deeps and
The bright white surface
Of my dark and bright
Zebra life, flesh barred,
Imprisoned:

This caged wild thing,
This gentle creature,
Like all the rest,
But quite unique,
She roamed,

Monochrome.
Alone in the veldt,
Tamed in the wild park,
Last of animal alphabet,
Omega replaced
By Zed.

Is she black barred on white,
Or white stripes on black?

Rainbows make me
New stripes, crazy
Candy-bar colours –
Un-camouflaged gaudy
Love's joke.

The black and white positive
To your white and black negative.
Picks rainbows from the dustbins of
Our past together,

Remembers so well our
Technicolor
Together times.

POEMS FOR A SICK CHILD

IMAGES

A friend's face, frightened, desperate, as I left the
Hospital where she awaited, fearfully, her
Surgery.

Dad's face, still, lifeless, yellow, cold. After my
Father had died; I washed and laid him out, flat in
His flat.

My son's face; thin, pale, fearful, angry, confused,
Sleepless; diagnosed, possibly wrongly,
Schizophrenic.

My face, grown weary, bags under eyes, wrinkled now
Though a weight of experience and pain taken in
This year.

Faces of friends, they ask if I'm O.K., It shows.
"Look after yourself," "God bless," "We are here,"
They say.

The face of my ex-spouse, that of a stranger. I feel
Compassion in a pain we share. It is rejected
Anyway.

The face of the dog, asleep beside the cat, both dreaming,
In their rem-sleep, paws twitch. I hope they at least are
Carefree.

I try to keep others from nightmares, but my strength
Is all but gone. Why so much pain? Life and love are a
Struggle.

The face of God, in changing seasons, in sunsets, in tears,
In laughter; Compassionate, but too often lidded from
Our view.

POEMS FOR A SICK CHILD

SCHIZOPHRENIA

"I will cut off my finger," he roars,
A knife in his hand, but he smiles.
"Would you mind if I killed myself?"
The samurai sword held to his stomach.

"I'm master of the Universe, I'm dead,
I don't exist" my son rambles on.
He's nothing, he's God, and he's frightened.

Voices mean he's lost, he's unhappy

This relentless, desperate illness,
Met with quiet words by me.
I remain exteriorly calm but
Scream my primal scream inside.

"It's exhausting!" I say, a knife in my heart.
I ask myself if he would mind if I walked away.
A smile, a teacup in hand, He's nothing.
He's gone. He's in his own universe

We don't exist. I smile; hold the teacup tightly
My child talks nonsense.
He's everything, Where is God?

I know he's lost. He's unhappy

This all-powerful illness is also destroying me
With his words.
I'm frightened
For him, not of him.

I want to protect him, to be able to help.
Inside me I weep and feel panic,
Seek calm but smile
To the outside world.

POEMS FOR A SICK CHILD

SPACED IN LOSS

His long blond hair hangs about his face
It is thin: eyes deep-set, medicated.
Drug-therapy does this as powerfully as the illness.

He is untidily dressed, trousers undone.
His trainers are too small, falling to bits.
There are stains on his jeans and tee-shirt.

He hasn't shaved the boyish fuzz from his chin.
Anger and pain, hysteria, false laughter,
Drowsiness, the trembling fingers, rocking:

Knees vibrating, hands gripping, sharp words
Roll out. He paces to and fro. He knows he's lost:
He wants answers, a cure for this feeling, NOW!

In the Park he demands attention, rejects advice.
Our dog, wagging his tail slowly stares at him,
He smells the same, he looks the same: but who is he now?

I WILL FLY

I will fly into that tree
And land high above you
All.

I am not small but tall.
I'll defend myself against
Them.

They say I'm mad because
I talk of my dreams of
Flight.

ON SECTION TOO

Ten people on section for their own protection.
Removed from society with their delusions,
Obsessions, crazy words, sadness, and illusions.

"The world has ended, I hold the key", one calls.
"Only one will be saved! It's up to me!" He falls.

A haven of insanity, a refuge from reality;
This psychiatric ward,
The 'best' the State will afford.

Patients beg for a "spare cigarette",
The locked doors; which are the staff?
Where is the Office?

Windows aren't barred, but wide
Open to a goldfish world outside.

Staff in the office, so much noise.
Patients pacing, dirty carpets,
Visitors trying to be calm,

Television on full blast.
Some sedated sleep at last,
Laid out by the medication cosh.

Matter of fact talk of Global Warming,
The Greenhouse Effect, The end game.

In a world we all help destroy.
Talk of love when so little is given.

Home to face the
Madness of the world outside.
Sectioned, set aside

* *It seems the world outside is just as mad as that of those inside on a "Section"*

POEMS FOR A SICK CHILD

PARK BENCH

I sit on a bench in the park with my son.
We have a cup of tea from the café,
And some chocolate. The sun is shining,
Warm for October. The dog sits quietly
Waiting for treats, his paw elevated to beg.
When the chocolate is gone he's off to explore.

My son, diagnosed schizophrenic, hair all askew,
Talks irrationally, shakes, paces up and down.
An old man asks if we mind if he sits on the bench...
We say we don't, but my heart sinks.
My son talks of the universe ending, of the
Need of 3 greens, 3 reds, and 3 blues to mix.

How it is he who decides whether it can go on, of the Planet
Venus, where he comes from, of flying through time...
His imagination and words of other patients, swirling
Through his confused head: The evil voices.
He gets angry at my gentle, quiet rationalisations,
Of words of hope and explanation, of exterior calm.

He goes off for a drink of water, without words.
I explain to the man, "He has had a nervous breakdown."
The man says he is sorry, but sits on in the sun
With us on the bench. The drama continues.
I feel drained by the madness and the sadness.
My son is both a child, who expresses his vulnerability,
And a lost angry man shows madness in his words and actions.

We say, "Goodbye" to the man, and walk off arm in arm,
Back to the unit where he is on Section"

"Will you come tomorrow?" My son asks.
"Yes" I say.

**When a sectioned person seems to be improving a period of supervised release is allowed. We used St Anne's Well Gardens, near to the Psychiatric Unit.*

POEMS FOR A SICK CHILD

SAFETY RAILINGS

He's dead. Jumped on an impulse.
Hit the safety railings. No rails round the roof.
Off the rails,

My arms not there to hold him.
Now I touch the railings, bowed, as I am,
By the impact.

A flight from pain, not from life,
His last journey. I can rail, in desolate
Angry weeping,

Screaming, regretting **"If only"** thoughts.
"If only
He'd phoned
I'd been there,
He'd been stopped,
It hadn't happened."

If only he'd missed the safety rails,
They'd be straight.
He would live.
I could catch him,
I could save him

And I wouldn't miss him,
Remembering a smile,
Not a fall.

Each of us must be free to fly,
Even without choosing a safety net,
Must I now build a safety rail
Round my heart and fear heights?

POEMS FOR A SICK CHILD

THE QUIET ROOM

I see him. Not a bed,
Not a table, on which he
Lies to attention.
He seems tall now,
Skin cooling,
Starting to blue.

I seek his hand,
Find it loose,
But clenched.
I see his grazed knuckles,
Touch those so long fingers.
So long,
My child.

Respectfully, they had put
Him in a hospital shroud,
As I have so many others,
Hating those plastic frills.
His face is calm above
The fresh white sheet,
Undamaged and quite still.

He needs a shave.
I carefully and with love
Tuck him in, this last time.
In the breathless silence
Now he asks no questions.
I have no answers.

Now I ask the questions.
It is complete.
He is dead.
I brush my son's hair.

* *Imagine a Nurse, a parent, who before had had to take other parents to the same Hospital's Quiet Room to see and say goodbye to their child who had died violently.*

POEMS FOR A SICK CHILD

PICTURES

We see friend's paintings in the gallery,
Brighton Festival has started.
Saw fireworks in the sea mist last night.
Glad my lover's by my side as she has been.

It is eight days since my son's death.
He'd have been with us on this day,
Seeing these pictures and sculptures.

Sharing his thoughts,
His ideas, and fears.
Both son and friend,
Musician and artist.

HOLDING THE FRAME

His painting is unfinished.
His life has no gallery,
But in the memories of friends
And in all those who love him.

Held in that frame
And in these hearts.
Well lit sometimes,
It is unfinished, others.

Glorious colours hang in memories.
In my head I hear a ragtime play,
I weep at the incongruity and
Tap my foot,

Seek his smile.

POEMS FOR A SICK CHILD

JUMPER

I wanted his jumper, to touch, to smell his scent,
A primitive reaction, a need to hold on to a life,
To those I love to see past the eyes and words
To him.

To know we feel the same and are they're together
For each other, in a way I know we cannot now be
For him

As children grow, we must learn to let them go
Yet be there, as we need and in case we too are
Needed.

But this, a sudden death, at this too early time
Of his so young promised life was unnatural,
Disordered.

It is a pain that rocks belief and sneaks up
Merciless, uninvited, only leaving such
Deep wounds.

As he leapt from his pain, towards his immortal life,
I'm conscious of my own mortality and
Vulnerability.

I celebrated his life with those who love him and I
Love. Yet in an empty place, I am not alone. I feel
Him close,

Sense his step,
Hear his music,
Smile

Sometimes.

POEMS FOR A SICK CHILD

MEETING THE SHADOW

At times I'm bridled and tethered by his going
By the walking and talking, tears and laughter
He and I shared,
My son.

He went too soon, now is freed from his pain.
This premature death leaves deep dismay, is a
Mistake,

But is it freedom he found? I miss his words and songs.
I see my shadow, in life, long in this autumn evening
Walking ahead or beside me, as he often
Once did.

My hand traces the ground, living fingers touching,
Meeting the shadow, as they held his, so still, hand,
That last and
Cruel time.

His life is gone; dreams and time are turned to ash.
I had hoped to meet his children, see them grow tall,
Like the oak tree we planted together on his
Birth-date.

Golden Flower Press

Belper - 2010